We had no fo
drinking water
and we had
shirts, and lifejackets to keep us
warm. The only piece of gear
either of us had left was our
river knives, clipped to our
life vests in the event we
had to free ourselves
from a fouled rope.
The Canyon was
getting darker,
and we had
run out of
options.

DEEP
BLACK

DEEP

AN ADVENTURE THROUGH

Western Reflections Publishing Company

BLACK

THE BLACK CANYON

Robb Magley

First Edition
Printed in the United States of America

ISBN 1-890437-68-9

Library of Congress Number 2002 104146

Western Reflections Publishing Company
P.O. Box 1647
Montrose, CO 81402-1647
www.westernreflectionspub.com

Cover and Book Design by Paulette Livers
Livers Lambert Design, Boulder, Colorado

I'm grateful for the help I've received in the creation of this book. Thanks to Paul Zaenger at the Black Canyon of the Gunnison National Park, for his time and dedication to history; Michael Brown for his unflagging faith and remarkable willingness to head off into the wild; And my wife Erin, without whom none of this would have been even remotely possible. I am indeed fortunate. —R.M.

I remember looking at pictures of Fellows and Torrence before we went in, and wondering what they were like. Couldn't help but think that a philosopher had at least as good a chance as a hydrologist loaded with surveying equipment. My hat's off to them. Still in the river, in fact.
—Michael Brown, 1998

I, *I have sometimes been asked if it paid and if I would undergo the same hardships again. My reply has always been "Yes," if the results to be obtained were so great as those which have followed this survey. When I think of the hardships, of the moments when there seemed to be no light ahead, when it appeared that the present moment was the last, I think, too, of the now prosperous towns in the Uncompahgre Valley, of the many happy homes, the beautiful orchards, the school houses filled with children, and I am content, knowing that out of trial, good cometh.*

—A. Lincoln Fellows, 1901

WHO WRITES HISTORY?

There is a school of thought which relegates historical inquiry to desks, archives, and cardboard boxes.

There is another which believes history to be a set of assumptions which remain insignificant if left untested. There exists a kind of historian who feels history's finest role is that of a springboard to contemporary adventure. One who feels a need to tell history's stories in terms that make sense to current-day readers, and in support of that need, realizes that it is not just history, but the story of the history which is most valuable.

Since we all know we're talking about me, I'll just explain:

In May of 1997, I backpacked into the Black Canyon of the Gunnison in Colorado, along with the woman who later that year (and despite her better judgment) acquiesced to become my wife. Erin and I had grown up as avid outdoorpersons, but it had been too long since either of us had been beyond city limits, so to speak. With visions of a recaptured childhood, we made the first of what would be many decisions together. We got out.

Erin's parents had begun building their dream house in Western Colorado in a tiny town near Telluride called Ridgway. In addition to a modest hot spring, Ridgway is best known (when it is known at all) as the filming location for much of the John Wayne classic, "True Grit." A few forward-thinking celebrities, escaping the inflated prices in Telluride, have built and are building vacation retreats in the hills surrounding town. Billed to me as a "cabin in the woods," my future in-laws' house was a surprising picture of comfort and convenience (the "cabin" I had created in my mind would have nestled snugly between the cars in the garage). Ridgway is the sort of delightful town where people still say hello on the street, where locals look at you with genuine concern if you don't remember to wave to the truck coming the other way. I noticed on my first visit its other wonderful quality: it felt like it was in the middle of nowhere.

The "cabin" was situated so that you didn't see your neighbors, unless you went looking for them (and brought a lunch). The view out the kitchen window was the stuff of design magazines, straight out across an aspen-laced valley towards a snow-capped mountain range. Looking on the map, there were National Forests everywhere, a rash of conservation across the face of the mining capital of the western world. Even where the wildness of an area wasn't implicitly protected by federal mandate, people in this region tended to own such enormous tracts that they couldn't possibly ruin it all in a lifetime. I became inspired, and my fever spread. My fiancee and I began prodding around, looking for a good place to explore it all.

In the formative years of my life (indeed, when do those truly end?), I had hiked, scrambled, kayaked and canoed through the Arizona and Utah canyonlands, following in the footsteps of the great desert-trudgers like Abbey, Butchart, and Fletcher. Canyon country, from the widest section of the Grand Canyon to the narrowest chute on the Paria, was my adopted home, and no matter how high a Rocky Mountain peak might reach, I had always felt it could never match the pure joy of finding a water pocket in red sandstone.

So, in my closed-minded fashion, I looked for another canyon for our trip. Erin and I cornered locals about opportunities to walk down a canyon in a state where wilderness is measured by counting 14,000 foot peaks. There was, as it turned out, one remarkable chasm worth mentioning: the Black Canyon of the Gunnison. Since we knew virtually nothing about it, except that it was a National Monument, it seemed ideal for the sort of life-affirming trip we had in mind. The next available long weekend, my future bride filled the pack she had carried through Europe, I borrowed her father's monstrous orange frame pack, we threw the pair in the bed of my sorely underpowered pickup, and made tracks for the Black Canyon of the Gunnison.

Just outside of Montrose, Highway 347 connected to South Rim Drive. Paved as it was, we were constantly finding ourselves trapped behind slow-moving Winnebegos, wheezing, belching monsters that held our speed to slower than we could walk. We were fresh from civilization, and like most vacationers before they actually get into their vacation, we were in a hurry. We raced towards the ranger station, pausing only briefly at a pull-off viewpoint, where we got our first look at the canyon below.

Neither of us had ever seen anything like it, and of course our minds couldn't find a reference for any of it. Distance, especially to someone used to staring no more than five feet ahead to the bumper of the next car, was impossible to gauge. You could read the signs, look at the contour lines on a topographic map; you could listen to the ranger describing the route you're planning to take. None of it meant anything, and in a moment of clarity (perhaps a foreshadow of feelings to come?) I understood that until we went down there, it was all just useless figures, more incomprehensible even than geologic time scales.

We had to get off that rim and into the depths. The ranger gave us directions to find the route I had chosen weeks before, staring at the map like a prisoner through bars. I had looked for the place where the descent was the most gradual, where the contour lines described a recognizable landscape, instead of crowding into a blur of solid brown. The topo map expressed the severity of the descent with its own elegance: "NOTE CONTOUR INTERVAL CHANGE NEAR MONUMENT: FROM 40 FEET TO 80." The route was known as the Warner Point Route, and it departed from the Warner Point Nature Trail (five feet wide but not yet wheelchair accessible) on its way towards the Warner Point Overlook, where one could, after a brief walk, see Warner Point itself.[1] If you were interested, that is, which we weren't; all we were searching for was the marked serviceberry bush, where we were told to turn left and begin our trip down.

"Marked?" I asked the ranger, wondering how a bush would be marked. Blaze-orange trail tape? A rock cairn? Three old-style hash marks on the thickest branch?

"Trust me," he said, "You'll see what I mean. You can't miss it."

And he was right, we didn't; this particular bush, out of tens of thousands on the rim, had been singled out to be the official National Park Service Serviceberry Bush, and was appropriately graced with a metal plaque. This not only informed the casual walker that yes, this was *ipso facto* a serviceberry bush, but also captivated hapless readers with a none-too-brief description of what a serviceberry bush was, where it grew, who used it for what, what bugs made a home of it, and so on. The facts beyond, that is to say, those that were apparent if you were standing right in front of the thing.

The descent began at a lovely saddle, between two smallish peaks. Wildflowers were just beginning their annual struggle, and from some hidden spot nearby came the scent of wild onions. We drank water, enjoyed the view, shouldered our weighty, overstuffed packs (we had planned a "gourmet," or damnably heavy, set of meals), and headed down.

It was the most grueling workout I could ever remember in the most beautiful place I had ever seen. We were both embarrassingly out of shape, carrying packs that were too

---

[1] This Warner, I remember thinking, must be an important fellow.

heavy for the physically fit, much less for us, on a route that dropped 2,700 feet in less than a mile. That last translates to "nearly straight down," in appreciable terms; each step was a halting, bone-jarring mini-leap of faith into the chasm. There were no good places to take off our packs and rest; the fear was that in the act of heaving our loads back onto our weary shoulders, the ensuing momentum would send us flying off our miserable and tiny perches into the abyss, down, down, reaching the river hours before our companion, days before rescue, broken and understandably upset. So we trudged on. A number of times my delirium got the better of me, and I offered to help my lovely fiancée by having her drop her backpack. I would head down a ways, drop my own pack, shuttle back up to get hers, scramble down with hers, park it, hoist my own back on, repeat until incredibly dizzy and no longer feeling chivalrous. Occasionally I would lower both our packs down some particularly steep section with an old piece of strap I carried, crouching and whipping the whole mess back and forth to dislodge it when some part hooked onto a tiny crag.

Seven and a half foolish hours later, we reached the river. Dazed, we had the briefest of moments to look around before darkness fell. Impressive canyon, we thought, particularly from the bottom, although each of us was privately thinking how it looked nearly as impressive from the top. We dropped our loads on the nearest sandbar, knocked the ticks from our waists (they seemed to like the sweaty section of my belly where my hip belt clung), made a hasty, non-gourmet dinner, threw together our tent, and passed out.

We spent the next day in one of my favorite wilderness pursuits, what a good friend of mine termed "power-lounging." This was ideal, despite our natural desire to explore the canyon floor, because our muscles were sore far beyond mere exhaustion. Our bodies were on sabbatical; there was nothing to do but wait as they did their best to repair damage we had inflicted the previous day.

It was during this day of what we will call "reflection" that I first appreciated the rhythm of this Canyon. Let me try to break it down:

Morning breaks, and the day passes largely uneventfully as the sun makes its short journey across our limited skyline, illuminating first one noble wall then the other before slipping again into obscurity. Then night starts to fall, and the dance begins—as if by simultaneous command, the flies that seemed immune to our repellent all day are gone. In their place arise mosquitoes, hundreds upon thousands of them swarming in the dying light.

The darting birds appear next, seemingly from nowhere and in equally impressive numbers, following the insects and one another in impossibly fast flight. As it becomes darker, and I start to wonder how they can possibly navigate, the birds are gone, and the click-click-click of the first of the bats begins to sound from every direction at once. The bats, far less sleek than the birds but reportedly ten times more efficient insect eaters, rise and fall upon invisible currents like drunken mice of the air, weaving back and forth, flapping madly forward and coming to full, stalling halts in mid-air before fluttering to gain necessary airspeed and bolting in another direction.

When the insects seem to be gone, the bats retire for the night, and before the moon appears there exists in the canyon a few moments of pure darkness. My instinct tells me everything waits out this period of befuddlement, but intellectually I know there are still more dramas to be played out, thousands of hunters and hunted continuing their own dances behind slotted night vision.

And we sat among it all, hopefully excluded from the game but affected by it in ways hard to put into words. I remember looking at the walls of that Canyon, wondering how it was seen by those who came before us, wondering about the history of the remote place we had come to by chance. We had been told by rangers that we were going into the "nicest" part of the Monument, because it had the longest stretches of accessible shoreline. "Accessible" has its own meaning in the Park Service; in most of the canyon, tiny sandbars are hemmed in by the barrier created when sheer cliff face meets raging river. But surely, I thought in the dark, some kind of person has been through, one end to the other?

Months later, from the comfort of my new home in Denver and the additional, immeasurable comfort of my new wife, I looked into the matter on a whim, thinking I could convince a good friend to journey down Black Canyon with me, and hoping I could sell the story of the trip as a magazine article. My friend, a Philosophy graduate student named Michael Brown, had other plans; ever the occupied academic, he couldn't quite spare the time to make the trek that year. In addition, with some serendipity, on the day he arrived for an all-too-brief visit, my query to a magazine I had chosen was rejected. Seeking solace, we wandered around downtown and I found myself killing time in the library, while Michael went to call on another friend.

Wasting time on the library computer, I ran a search for any books in the system with the word "wilderness" in the title or subject. Several thousand entries came back to me and, having nothing better to do, I scrolled down the list. Among the texts concerning cooking and survival were works about the Black Canyon of the Gunnison. Narrowing my search, I found a dozen listings; nearly all of them were books I had already seen in preparation for my article query.

Except for one.

A listing appeared for an unpublished manuscript, in the Western History section of the library, available with assistance only. It was a set of documents titled "Papers, 1892-1934," by Abraham Lincoln Fellows, a man I knew to be one of the first two men to successfully navigate the Black Canyon. They performed the feat, I had read previously, in 1901, a date that fell squarely inside the boundaries of these "papers." I knew I had to read them, learn more about this man and the Canyon he had, for all practical purposes, "discovered." I did not, however, anticipate that I would develop an interest in the history of Black Canyon that bordered on (some say clearly violated the sovereignty of) obsession.

The book you now hold is the story of my research, such as it was, whether poring intently over hundred-year-old documents or staring bewildered at billion-year-old rocks. I wanted to get inside the man who had "made it," if it meant hours in a manuscript room or days in the backcountry. And that's what this story is about. Knowing what it's about, that's a start; and every journey, they say, begins with a tiny, hesitant first step. . . .

2.

LIBRARIES ARE BIG.

Some are bigger than others, obviously. Denver's downtown wonder is a multiple-story design-school affair, with more within its walls than anyone could digest in a lifetime. With that kind of size, it struck me as no wonder that there are scores of people who devote their entire lives to the organization, if not direct study, of every word of it. This task is formidable, and I mention it in passing only to underscore one remarkable fact: in all my previous computer-aided searches for things written specifically about the Black Canyon, I never came across any hint that the Fellows papers existed.

That being said, my elation in finding this little historical gem was tempered by some of the words in its description. "Ask for assistance" was the first to give me pause, my being of the shy sort who would much rather write a letter to a stranger than actually speak to them. Electronic mail for me is nothing more or less than another excuse to avoid the telephone. As if that wasn't enough, there was another phrase that, well, frightened me:

"Open to all qualified researchers."

Qualified? I had no doubt that if anyone with half a brain were dividing the people in the library into "qualified" and "hack," I would fall neatly into the group asked to wait by the pay phone while the others did their work. Even the term "researcher" worried me; was that what I was? Researchers were looking for cancer cures; I was just curious about some turn-of-the-century adventurer who explored a canyon I wandered into once.

Returning home I voiced my concerns to my academic friend Michael, who informed me that, yes, often archival personnel do require proof of the validity of your research. He recommended I 1) wear a nice pair of slacks and 2) smile and let whoever was behind the desk do all the talking.

The next day, feeling something between a thief and an impostor, I made my way to the fifth floor with neatly printed index card in hand. I approached the desk and was confronted, not by a spindly woman in her mid-eighties, but by a young man who, by his dress, demeanor, and facial hair, clearly identified himself as a contemporary of my friend Michael: the North American graduate student.

I stepped to the plate: "Good morning, I was wondering if I could take a look at this," and I pushed my card into his face.

One moment's pause; I thought the jig was up ("Oh, well," he would say, "this is *really* indescribably valuable and unique, quite old. Could you tell me where you received your doctorate?").

"Hm," he actually said. "Well, this is in the back stack, and it requires a 24-hour wait. Would that be all right?"

I stifled the urge to do back flips and nodded, proceeding to fill out a short request form.

That evening was like Christmas Eve, and I felt the need to celebrate and boast of my subterfuge. My wife and I visited some friends in their new house for dinner, and I prattled on about how exciting my life had become, how I was going to do "research" on some long dead adventurer through his "papers," only open to those who were "qualified," which now included me. The wind was let only slightly from my sails when I discovered that one of my hosts, in the course of his daily work identifying local historic buildings, regularly visited the archival section of the library and, to my disappointment, found it anything but intimidating or exciting.

No matter; one man's meat, and so on. I sipped my wine and stayed mostly silent for the rest of the evening, content with the personal conviction that I was on the verge of something great.

2.

TRUTH BE TOLD, there were quite a few things I knew about the Black Canyon before I even set foot in the archives.

First, I knew why it's known as Black Canyon. It has often been referred to as "The Grand Canyon of the Gunnison," the name it was given by map-makers in the 1880s, although this is not quite correct. Early mapping efforts named the narrowest stretches below the mouth of the Cimarron River "Black Canyon," placing it squarely within the "Grand" canyon. "Grand" canyon, because it was at the time known as the "Grand" river. Before that, trappers called it the "Blue," and local tribes referred to it as "Nahunkahrea." This length, what I call "the Canyon," is so tall, narrow, and dark that sunlight rarely exposes much of it at any one time. Indeed, a quite Black Canyon.

Second, that it is now and has been for all time one of the most inaccessible places in the nation. Long before the first pale face peered into its depths and let out the same long, slow whistle they usually reserved for a train derailment, the Ute Indians discovered it and decided to stay away. A quite sensible tribal tradition held that no man could enter it and come out alive; as a result, the only archeological evidence of people living anywhere nearby is found on the rim.

Southwestern history buffs will recall that in 1776, while our founding fathers were hashing out a new nation far to the East, two Franciscan priests were trying to discover a trade route between missions in Santa Fe and those in California. Padres Silvestre Velez de Escalante and Francisco Antanasio Dominguez were intrepid travelers and mapmakers, if poor missionaries; their attempts to convert the Utes they met en route failed miserably. The tribal leaders were kind enough to lend the wanderers a guide, who led them right out of the state without visiting the Canyon, passing within ten miles of today's park boundary.

Current theory holds that the first non-natives to see the Black Canyon were French beaver trappers. Although there is no written record of the first encounter between white man and chasm, it seems likely one of the first was a trapper named Antoinne Robidoux.[2] Robidoux was something of a frontier entrepreneur, and in the 1830s he constructed and operated a trading post nearby. Film-goers may recall a "Fort Rubidoux" in the opening scenes of "Jeremiah Johnson," starring Robert Redford. Same place. Utes burned his post to the ground in 1837, and the Black Canyon remained substantially unexplored for some time.

Rumors of gold had first brought the Spanish to this area; now similar rumors of the metal in California brought people in the East to demand an easier way to get there. Enter the Army Corps of Engineers; their orders were to survey a

---

[2] One book claims the Canyon was discovered in 1809 by a pair of unnamed trappers, possibly contemporaries of Robidoux.

railroad, and to do it they enlisted the aid of Captain John Williams Gunnison to find a route through southern Colorado. Gunnison mistook Tomichi Creek (a tributary of what is now known as the Gunnison River) for the Colorado River somewhere above the Black Canyon, and he followed it. As the terrain worsened, he wisely determined that this was no place for a railroad, and climbed out, neatly circumnavigating the canyon.

Although he was shortly thereafter killed by Paiutes in Utah, Gunnison's contributions did not go unnoticed in the region; the river bears his name, as do both a county, a town, and a sizable National Forest. Further, the railroad was eventually built, and prospectors headed for the hills of California in droves.

California, however, did not have nearly enough gold to go around, and by the late 1850s those droves of now quite poor prospectors headed back East. Since they had already bought mining gear, some of them stopped and poked around in Colorado, managing to strike it rich there. By the 1870s, the southwestern part of the state was, quite literally, a gold mine, and new surveys and additional rail lines were demanded.

The 1874 geological survey expedition led by Ferdinand Hayden is remembered as a wonderfully successful trip, if for no other reason than that no one was killed off by Indians. In fact, Hayden's tribal nickname translated to "white man who picks up rocks while running," a fairly accurate if overly precise moniker for a geologist. Hayden's group could hardly have missed the Black Canyon, and did a great deal of mapping from the rim, correctly believing that it was much, much easier than mapping from the bottom. Supposedly, at one point, they lowered some hapless surveyor into the depths with a 1,000 foot long rope, then hauled him back up. Not surprisingly, he found the experience disagreeable, and taking his emphatic advice the team stayed on the rim.

Around 1881, a railroad was completed nearby, and although it followed the river religiously for most of its trek through the region, the route climbed out of the canyon near the present park and missed the worst of it. The rail ascent was quite steep, and took a number of engines to pull a load of any weight; annoyed by the inconvenience, the railroad company hired another team of surveyors to map out the as yet unexplored lower region.

Planning for a twenty-day expedition, it comes as no great surprise that sixty-five days later, a frozen and mildly starving team of mapmakers (led by one Byron H. Bryant) emerged from the canyon area and recommended to bag the whole idea. They did successfully survey the depths, but had climbed out at every available opportunity; in fact, nearly every night.

By 1900, no one had yet made it through the entire length of the canyon along the bottom. Prompted by local farmers clamoring for more water, some enterprising engineers declared it mathematically possible to divert water from the Gunnison River to the surrounding valley.[3] The only obstacles were that a) the tunnel would have to go through nearly six miles of rock, and b) no one had any appreciable knowledge about the part of the Canyon where the engineers wanted to start digging.

It was, however, the turn of the century in America, and "can-do" prevailed over "what-in-hell-are-you-thinking."

---

[3] The idea for this water diversion is usually attributed to a French miner-cum-settler in the region named Lauzon. He disappears from most accounts once the engineers arrive.

Engineers were the miracle workers, and the workers themselves worked cheap. So, following the wisdom of the engineers and no doubt thinking of their farming constituency, the Colorado Senate gave their blessing to five men who headed into the canyon with wooden boats, surveying equipment, and a hearty handshake.

This expedition was led by John E. Pelton, who brought with him four other men including the local Power and Light superintendent, one William W. Torrence (more on him later). Although seemingly well-supplied, this trip was doomed to what will be by now a predictable failure. After covering about fifteen miles in a month, they gave up the ghost and returned home; the Black Canyon had prevailed yet again.

Looking back into the gorge, Torrence named the point of the team's departure the "Falls of Sorrow." Perhaps more fitting would have been the name, "Falls of Determination," for he spent the next year doing little else but planning for a second attempt on the Canyon.

The Colorado State Engineer's Office, which by this time shared many goals (and a stenographer) with the Reclamation Department, liked the idea of a diversion tunnel so much that they sent their most promising young hydrographer to join Torrence in a final, and ultimately successful attempt on the Black Canyon.

If you hadn't guessed it, that man was Abraham Lincoln Fellows.

4

I STEPPED OFF THE ELEVATOR on the fifth floor, not entirely sure I was in the right place. Then I glanced at a glass case in the center of the lobby: I beheld a bit of Americana, a Remington bronze sculpture, one of many depicting a horseman barely keeping himself on a bucking bronco. This had to be it.

Through one metal detector, then another. The two boxes would be waiting for me. And they were, although it took me nearly half an hour to find them. I was lucky enough to be helped by perhaps the nicest librarian I had met so far.

She gave me a quick smile. "They're remodeling the walls, or something . . . and they're refinishing the tables."

"Will I still get to sit down?"

"Probably."

Finally the boxes were in front of me, and there on the side, in some hurried archivist's script, were the words,

FELLOWS, ABRAHAM LINCOLN 1864-1942
PAPERS, 1892-1934

Just the thing.

My notebook having been confiscated at the front desk (to cut down on pilfering, I supposed), I sat with my loose paper and dull pencil briefly savoring the moment of discovery. As silly as it now seems, I did have a moment where I felt like what sat before me would herald the end of my little journey. I unwrapped the string holding the first box shut, lifted the lid, and began pawing through the contents, doing my best to look as if I was handling the hundred year-old documents with practiced care.

Inside the first box were a number of medium-sized envelopes, all open and standing on end. Inside each, I could see little black books, scarcely larger than an address book, each of those with a different color on the edge of the paper. Some were rimmed with gold leaf, some were multicolored, speckled, and a few toward the front were simply edged with the yellow stain of time.

These last, as noted on their envelopes, were the oldest, beginning with a little book from 1892. At the back of the box was one marked "1914." Complete, as advertised, nicely organized so that even an idiot like myself couldn't mess it up too badly.

I opened the first of twenty-two volumes, representing twenty-two years of a man's life. I remember wondering how someone could keep the strength of conviction to dutifully record the day's events every day, for twenty-two years. What made him start? What made him stop? Eight thousand and thirty entries, plus three more to take care of the leap years. And every day, he forced himself to think of something meaningful to say.

Or rather, as it turned out, he didn't; it wasn't long before I realized that the texts I had before me were no diaries, no articles of confession. I was not going to discover a secret love, or remarks on an interesting cloud; these papers would not bring me to the heart of the man. What I was holding amounted to discovering someone's dayplanner.

I had forty-two years of brief, single-line accounts of Fellows' daily location and occupation. My heart sank as I flipped pages, each day virtually indistinguishable from the next. I pulled out the book from the year of his greatest achievement (1901, to my way of thinking), and found, as an example:

> *January 1: Day was spent in part at the office and in part at home. New Year's Dinner at Lackners'; Mr. Prall staying with us."*

Most days, I found, were spent in part at the office and in part at home. Office more in the daytime, and evenings at home. Not exactly ground breaking.

> *January 2: Very cold weather. Day spent in office, read part of* Midsummer's Night's Dreams. *[sic]*

Aha! I thought, perhaps a man of letters! Or at least someone who understood the value of doing as little work as possible in the office; I began to feel a bond forming.

> *January 3: Day spent in office.*

Doing what? Thinking what?

January 4: Office work.

What kind of office work? What exactly is it you do? Was it difficult? Easy?

January 5: Office work.

Was it your own idea to do the work? What were you thinking about when you looked away from it, towards the window? Did you even have a window? Did you have dinner with a friend after work, a few drinks? Did he ask you how your day was? What did you say? What did you mean?

January 6 (Sunday): At Church and Mission.

A religious man! Were you satisfied with the sermon? Was there a woman across the room, snug in her winter coat, whose rosy cheeks and shivering lips made you lose track of what was being said? Did you shake hands with the pastor?

January 7: In office.

Arrgh! Doing what?

January 8: In office.

And so on. I scanned ahead, looking for significant change. There really wasn't any to speak of; in his nearly illegible scrawl, Fellows dutifully recorded his whereabouts and, on rare occasions, something substantive of what he was doing *("working on resolutions for legislature. . . . examine reservoir sites. . . . meet with Mr. _____,"* etc.). He never mentioned why he was somewhere, what drove him to be doing something, or what he thought of the matter when given a chance. These documents, possibly a means of tallying his deeds for his monthly expense account sheet, were as dry as the desert he sought to reclaim. Vapid. Impersonal.

It seemed I wouldn't be in danger of feeling the research was too easy. As a qualified researcher, apparently I would have to do more research. I would have to sleuth a bit, ferret out a little about the man from what I had in front of me. Infer, try to put meaning into the humblest scraps of peoples' lives. Elementary, my dear Watson. "Now what kind of man were you, Abraham?"

That he would be full of attention to detail seemed almost a foregone conclusion. He was, after all, an engineer; outside of the church, his God was found lurking in the details. My man Fellows was meticulous, for certain; that much was clear just from looking at the consistency of entries. There were even duplicates of one year; it seemed as if he had misplaced his book for a few months, and purchased a new one. Once he had found his old one again, he filled in the missing months in both books. In a strange way, I was impressed.

I skipped around the books a bit, picking them up at random, doing what I call Zen research. I scanned the pages, the inside covers, the margins, looking for shreds of the man trapped inside the engineer. In the 1902 book, somewhat nicer than the others (leather-bound; a gift?), I found a page titled, "Things Easily Forgotten," not in his handwriting, but put there by the printer, much like the modern "Important Phone Numbers."

Fellows had, as a dutiful owner of this slightly nicer book, filled out each space to the best of his ability:

No. of Watch Case: 9033
No. of Works: 8462

For repairs, presumably; or was it in case of loss or theft?

No. of Bicycle: 67106

That one seems to definitely be for theft. Was bicycle thievery rampant in the turn-of-the-century west? I made a note to see if I could find out.

My Weight on January 1, 1902: 150 lbs.
My Height: 5 ft. 8 in.

Not a small man, by any standards, especially those in the 1900s, but by no means a hulking brute of the type expected to be out braving the wilderness in unknown canyons. My thoughts turned to John Wesley Powell, the bearded, one-armed war hero who led an expedition to map the Grand Canyon some years before Fellows' journey down the Black. Powell was crippled, and not particularly young; yet he endured and triumphed, much to the amazement of his colleagues.

But Powell had considerable bulk to him; my man seemed ill-fitted for roughing it. 150 pounds doesn't go very far in the backcountry, especially in the days of wet leather and cast iron skillets.

Size of my Hat: 7 1/8
Size of my Gloves: 8
Size of my Hosiery: 10
Cuffs: 10 Drawers: 33 Shirt: 37
Size of my Shoes: 7

I made another note to make up a suit of clothes to Fellows' measurements, then try it on. Then I had the wisdom to cross out that thought; that was probably taking it a bit too far. I revised the idea, vowing to attempt to walk a mile in size 7 shoes. Perhaps at some point in the idler days of my life.

Now I had a few vital statistics about Fellows, and a picture of the man was beginning to form in my mind. But I was still looking for the spark, the core, the part of him that aspired to explore new frontiers. Where would I find it?

Continuing to flip, a folded piece of card stock fell from one of the books. I examined it; it seemed to be an engraved invitation and, in a small way, the first evidence that men like Fellows were not all business.

Mr. A.L. Fellows;
You are cordially invited to be present at
(a probable safe distance of about a mile from)
"Dam Site"
at West Beaver Creek, Teller County, Colorado
at two o'clock p.m.
Dec. 18th, 1899
to participate in an explosion of
"Vesuvius Butte"
kindly bring your Kinetoscope and Accident Policy

If you're wondering what a Kinetoscope is, I didn't know either, and had to look it up in Webster's: "A device for viewing through a magnifying lens a sequence of pictures on an endless band of film moved continuously over a light source and a rapidly rotating shutter that creates an illusion of motion."

This was engineer humor at its best, a combination of the pride in beginning new work, a healthy realization of the dangers involved in their everyday lives, and the giddy excitement of a bunch of men about to blow something up. I knew it well; my own father was a Mechanical Engineer from the University of Washington, and I remembered one of his few jokes:

The engineer runs to the President of the U.S., waving a piece of scrap paper and warning that this was the day that California was going to break off and slide into the sea. So the President boards Air Force One, and circles over the fault line waiting for events to unfold. At the prescribed time, all watch as everything east of California slides into the sea. When the President stares accusingly at the engineer, his response is 'Damn, I misplaced a minus sign.'

Comedy at its simplest and most exclusive; only people who do that kind of work think it even remotely amusing. I was beginning to enjoy the company of Mr. Fellows.

There was further evidence, in the back of the 1899 book, that Fellows had a sense of humor, or at least held a taste for the peculiar. Scribbled in the very back, on a page intended by the printer for "Memoranda," Fellows had written a few lines entitled "Puzzles." And that is exactly what they were to me, inexplicable little snips of language that doubtless had meaning for him, though held little for me.

Puzzles:
State Engin Neere
Retail Spirits
Well Red Man
A. Virgin, Blacksmith. Work of all kinds done promptly.
Take one, chinaman.

These must have been things Fellows had thought of or heard in his travels or at work. The first a childish play on words, the second perhaps meant to display the irony of selling ghosts? "Well Red Man" is clearly another play on words, and the "A. Virgin" bit reminded me again of my father, and his inability often to remember enough of a joke to successfully retell it. But "Take one, chinaman" remained beyond my grasp. Perhaps Fellows, like a few of my own friends, merely had to tell the punch line to a previously told joke to get a laugh out of a crowd: "Rectum? Nearly killed 'em!" Somehow I doubted it, however. That didn't seem like my man.

Remembering briefly my initial focus, I decided to pore over the 1901 book to see if I could find evidence of the historic trip down the Black. By May's entries, the nearby town of Montrose began to be mentioned quite often, and finally a reference to the Gunnison River Diversion Tunnel:

May 18: to Cimarron, then on to Montrose. Met several people concerning the Gunnison Tunnel.

May 28: Meet Fitch [Charles Hall Fitch, topographer in charge of Fellows' division in the northwestern U.S.], to Montrose, there meet those interested in Gunnison Survey.

And then, a reference to seeing the gorge. I suspected it was not Fellows' first time looking into the Black Canyon, but I still believed it made an impact:

May 29: Visit GUNNISON CANYON.

This entry was written in uncharacteristically large and flowing script; perhaps he realized what a momentous occasion, or place, it was.

After that, Fellows returned to Denver and his office, taking care of other business, and attended the "Trans-Mississippi Congress" at Cripple Creek. On June 20th, he returned to Montrose with another superior, who toured the Gunnison survey site. With as full a dance card as ever, Fellows did not remain long, and hurried back to Denver for several meetings and planning sessions concerning a number of projects.

On the 10th of August, he made it back to Montrose and, after a two-day trip to Telluride and Delta, entered the Black Canyon with W.W. Torrence to begin his historic trip. The enormity of the event remained, as I expected, unreflected in the pages of this book:

August 12: Start for Grand Canyon Gunnison with Torrence.
August 13: In Gunnison.

August 14: Reach boat landing at night.[4]

August 15: Reach boat landing.["at" was crossed out to put "reach"]

August 16: Resume trip.

August 17: En route.

August 18: Reach Red Rock [this is crossed out]

August 19: Reach Red Rock after 1/2 day.

August 20: Red Rock to Black Canyon.

August 21: Return to Montrose.

August 22: In Montrose and on train for Denver.

Turn-of-the-century folks seemed to often interchange "Grand Canyon of the Gunnison" with "Black Canyon of the Gunnison," so there was no surprise there. And I knew Red Rock Canyon to be the last major tributary canyon inside the present National Park, a likely place to walk out of the Black and make for civilization. But what happened each day? Why were things crossed out? Did Fellows and Torrence think they had reached Red Rock a day earlier than they did? Did they try a wrong side canyon and have to return to the river, still trapped by the walls of stone? And why was the trip "resumed" on the 16th? Was there an interruption of some sort?

Clearly, these little books weren't going to tell me. I stuffed them back into their respective envelopes, put those back into the box, and closed it, fuming. I had the bones, but no meat.

---

[4] Boat landing, as I would eventually figure out from old photographs, was the name for the point where "Trail Gulch" meets the Gunnison River. This was the spot where the Gunnison Tunnel eventually began, where the short-lived construction town of Lujane sprang up, and where today's visitor finds East Portal.

In the second box I found two things I was interested in. The first was a letter to someone named "James"; what made the letter interesting was that it had a title. It was called "A History of the Year 1901"; this sounded like something I wanted to read thoroughly, so I bookmarked it to photocopy later. The second thing I discovered was a set of poems, collected and bound by a family member long after Fellows passed on. It seemed that when he wrote poetry, he referred to himself as "Aleph," a play on his initials "A.L.F." Most of the verses seemed to be inspirational, and all of them were rhyming. Among these, I found one entitled "The River." It seemed appropriate to get a copy of that as well.

It was getting late; Erin walked into the archives, looking exhausted from her day. I quickly reassembled the boxes, got my copies made, and left for home.

S,

I SAT ON MY PORCH and read "The River" by A.L. Fellows:

> From the heart of the grand old mountains,
> Where the golden sunlight falls
> On a lovely, flower-decked valley
> Girt 'round by granite walls,
> Springs a dancing, sparkling rivulet
> Born of the snows on high
> That lie on the glistening hillsides,
> Where hardly e'en birds dare fly.
>
> And, leaping into the sunlight,
> Forth through the valley it flows,
> Bearing refreshment and gladness
> To the flowers wherever it goes;
> And, joining in play with its sisters,
> And bubbling over with fun,
> It becomes a beautiful river,
> Fair daughter of Ocean and Sun.

Now down through the mountain meadows
It winds in its sinuous way,
While under its heaving bosom
Dart the trout in merriest play;
Always rippling with laughter
Except that 'tis sad when the sun
Withdraws his face, and the shadows
Proclaim that the day is done;

Or when clouds cover the mountains
With a shade of deepening gloom,
Or the distant, muttering thunder
Seems to tell of a threatening doom,
Then changed is the streamlet's nature
And it sluggishly creeps along,
And stilled is its merry laughter
And hushed is its bubbling song.

But as soon as the storm is over
And the sun peeps forth once more,
Then glad again is the water
And again with a rush and a roar,
It hastens away on its mission,
O'er its path to the mighty sea,
Refreshing all as it passes,
From flower to loftiest tree,

But again comes a change in its nature,
For now through a canyon dark
It plunges in gloom and in tumult,

Away from the sunlit park;
And for miles of its course it labors
Over boulders huge and gray,
Like a weary, toilworn mortal
O'er the obstacles in his way.

But at last it leaps with gladness
From the canyon's gloomy caves,
Greeting once more the sunshine
And tossing its sparkling waves;
And again through the sunlit valleys
It hastens with joy, once more,
Eager to join with its kindred
On the Ocean's golden shore.

It seems to me that the river
Is a symbol of human life,
Passing from childhood's sunshine
(With its fleeting moments of strife)
On to manhood's toil and labor,
With its hope of peace at the last,
Inviting the wearied homeward
To where anger and strife are past.

And I hope that, after the tumult,
When the autumn of life is at hand
And I'm reaching the end of my journey,
I may find such a peaceful land;
And I pray that, after the sorrows
And labors of life are o'er,

I, too, may find peace with my loved ones
On Eternity's golden shore.

A footnote to the text, added by one of Fellows' descendants, mentions that he used to read this poem at the conclusion of lectures he gave concerning the Gunnison Tunnel, showing slides of pictures from his historic trip. I tried to imagine the reactions of the engineers and local politicians, come to the lecture to learn about water diversion, presented with flowery images of the life of a river.

I imagined many of them could not get much past the spectacle of ending a scientific lecture with a poem. Certainly, a few were intrigued, especially in light of the peculiar nature of Fellows' trip down the Gunnison. It struck me suddenly that the trip must have had a profound effect on Fellows, that at some point and for some unknown length of time after, the journey became less a scientific exploration than a parallel to a man's life, with its good times and bad.

I wondered how long that feeling lasted.

6,

"A REVIEW OF THE YEAR 1901" turned out to be a remarkable find in my search, because it contained the first eyewitness account (if in its brevity it could be so labeled) of the trip I had yet come across. In the few books I had found on the Black Canyon, only enough details were provided about Fellows' trek to whet my appetite, and those details seemed so shaky as to make me suspicious of their accuracy. I had decided that when checking facts, or deciding if "facts" were true, I would assume a written account to be accurate only if every date and event jibed with the primary sources I had (e.g., Fellows' writings). If one fact or story was wrong, the whole piece became suspect. The idea was that this kind of severity would help me learn what actually happened.

So "Review" was an important text for me to see, and as such I read it on my front porch. I found inside evidence that Fellows was an accomplished writer, or at least had an extremely competent secretary to edit his work. Since he seemed to give so many well-received lectures, I assumed the former; further, since so much of what I found in "Review" seemed to reflect a personal wit well fueled by an educated and sharp mind, I felt it probably represented the man himself.

He speaks well and interestingly about one of his associates, C. T. Prall, in this letter addressed to "James":

> You never knew Mr. Prall, did you? Well, you have missed a good deal in your life. . . . It was more fun than a box of monkeys just to have him about.

Remarks about government:

> The memorable (for its incompetency) Thirteenth General Assembly was in session; J. B. Orman and a fusion rabble having been elected the preceding fall to (theoretically) fill the various offices . . . I had several interesting experiences with His Excellency (?) Governor J. B. Orman . . .

Some dark humor concerning a trip he took early in the year:

> . . . That Arkansas trip, by the way, is one of the kind which makes one want to choke his grandmother . . .

And then, on the fifth page, Fellows begins to write about the conditions surrounding his trip down Black Canyon:

> For some time I had been working in behalf of the so-called Gunnison project; namely, an undertaking having reference to the diversion of the waters of the Gunnison into the Uncompahgre Valley, which would require a tunnel of unknown length from a canyon of unknown difficulties.

The remark "so-called Gunnison project" surprised me somewhat; it was almost as if Fellows was expressing a lack of confidence in the tunnel's feasibility. That seemed unusual to me, chiefly because this letter was written after he had made his journey; he had already determined that the Black Canyon (or the "Grand Canyon") of the Gunnison was passable, and the tunnel itself a possibility. I concluded that although the letter came after his trip, it still preceded the actual tunnel construction by nearly a decade; it was and is an engineer's style to err on the side of caution, whether with figures or opinions.

What followed were two paragraphs which represented what I considered to be the only trustworthy account of the trip I had yet located. As with his short-winded daybooks, the telling of the tale was brief; perhaps this was just more of the engineer's predisposition towards understatement. In Fellows' words:

Upon the 12th [of August], accompanied by Mr. W. W. Torrence, I started down the Gunnison Canyon from Cimarron, and after ten days of the hardest kind of labor, clambering over the huge boulders, swimming the river seventy odd times, scaling the sides of cliffs and resting only when it was too dark to travel, we succeeded in getting through, returning to Montrose from Delta upon August 21st. There were times when we thought we would never get out, when we had to turn back and try other ways, and times when death seemed certain. In one place we were over half a day in making less than a quarter of a mile, and in another place we had to retrace our steps and spent the night just across the river from where we had been at noon.

All that backtracking and loss of momentum must been frustrating for Engineer Fellows. He went on to tell a mini-story about the trip:

> Upon one occasion I had the misfortune of falling some twenty feet, but received no serious injury. A mountain sheep was less fortunate, for it was so startled when it saw me that at the first spring it fell off and was killed.

Now this was interesting: a slightly comical story about a mountain sheep, an anecdotal tale about man interacting with foolish wildlife. This caught my attention because it seemed like such a unique and charming tale. Fellows concludes:

> However, all difficulties were safely overcome, and the trip may be considered a success in every way. . . . and all the information was gained that could have been expected. We, or rather Mr. Torrence, was received with open arms upon his return to Montrose, and neither of us will ever regret the trip.

Reading this paragraph, the word "grace" entered my mind for the first time. There was in Fellows a certain dignity, a nonchalant air about the way he told a story, that filled me with honor at having been given his time. I began to see Fellows' reticence and lack of severe emotive reaction as less a sign of an unimaginative mind, as I could no longer ignore the evidence of the poetry, than of a kind of quiet decency, a gallant serenity that reflected a man who had seen much, and been bothered by little.

Still, I had very few hard facts relating to events that took place during the trip. I knew when they went in, when they came out, that it was difficult, that a sheep expired, and that they emerged more or less uninjured. I sat back on the porch with my copy of "Review," and tapped it against my leg. The two boxes of papers had proven somewhat revealing, but it didn't seem enough to do justice to either the man or the importance of the trip. I needed more, but I had no idea where to find it.

I have mentioned before the concept of Zen research, of letting your fingers (or mind) do the sorting without any out-side assistance and eventually letting the facts fall into place. As the masters say, you may not get where you were heading, but you're bound to end up where you're supposed to be. If you believe in this sort of thing, you are likely to appreciate what happened next.

I was up against what felt like a brick wall. I was out of material, and had no idea where to find more. So I did what all good people do when confronted with an insurmountable obstacle: I ignored it. Utterly. I read newspapers, tidied the house, did anything I could think of waiting for someone or something to deliver me beyond my impasse.

As I was cleaning out a stack of folded maps and papers that had accumulated over the summer in my backpack, I found the map the Park Service had given Erin and me at the ranger station in the Black Canyon National Monument. I smiled, unfolded it, and reminisced for a moment or two. Then I decided to read it, give it a better look than I had when I hastily stuffed it into a pocket. On the front, overlaying a fantastic photo of the chasm, was printed a quote from none other than Abraham Lincoln Fellows:

Our surroundings were of the wildest possible description. The roar of the water . . . was constantly in our ears, and the walls of the canyon, towering half mile in height above us, were seemingly vertical. Occasionally a rock would fall from one side or the other, with a roar and crash, exploding like a ton of dynamite when it struck bottom, making us think our last day had come.

I was astounded. This was descriptive language, exciting language, describing a particular scene and Fellows' reaction to it all. My heart was in my throat; I knew this quote had to come from somewhere. And I had another lead to follow.

1.

IT TURNED OUT TO BE MORE DIFFICULT to call the Black
Canyon of the Gunnison National Monument than I had
thought. First, the phone number printed on the map was
incorrect. Looking it up in a guide book, I discovered that the
last two digits had been switched. Dialing that number, I was
told by a machine that the visitor center was under renovation,
and for emergencies I should call 911, which I considered, or
for other business I should call the headquarters building.

This was approaching a level that was more than a tele-
phone-shy person like myself could bear, but I managed to
reach someone quite helpful at the headquarters building. He
listened patiently to my prattling request for information, then
referred me to another number where there was someone who
might be able to help me. At wit's end, I called that number and
finally routed myself into the person's voicemail, where I left a
plaintive message about what I was looking for, and a request
that he return my call whenever he had a moment.

Not two hours later, I received a call back from a remarkable man named Paul. Paul was not remarkable because he

was smart, polite, considerate, or even a ranger; Paul's singularity rose out of his interest in Abraham Lincoln Fellows.

We spoke for nearly an hour, and I couldn't have been more pleased. Paul had been trying for some time to get a story together about that first trip, with limited success.

"People ask," he said, "and we just don't have good answers for them. Especially if they ask detailed questions."

So Paul had taken on the task of assembling records of Fellows, Torrence, and the Black Canyon in some good order. He had no idea where the quote on the map had come from; apparently its source was part of his mission.

"We have so many seasonal workers, and so few of them leave a good paper trail."

After we laughed about the stiffness and odd wit of Fellows' writing, as he had read "A Review of the Year 1901" through another source, Paul agreed to send me photocopies of five articles he had found dating from 1903 to 1938 about Fellows and the trip, and I promised to send him copies of Fellows' poems.

A few days later, I received the articles in the mail, and began looking them over. They were, in chronological order, "The Gunnison Tunnel," by A. L. Fellows (1903, *Forestry and Irrigation*), "Exploring the Gunnison Cañon," by C. H. Forbes Lindsay (1907, *World's Work Magazine*), "The Heroes of the Gunnison Tunnel," by A. W. Rolker (1909, *Everybody's Magazine*), "Interesting People: A. Lincoln Fellows," by George Creel (1911, *The American Magazine*), and finally, "America's No. 1 Water Boy," by Frank C. Cross (1938, *Western Farm Life*).

All of the articles, which were kept in an archive Paul supervised, had their own particular slants. I don't mean to say simply that each writer was concerned with his own interests, for clearly that also was the case; for example, Fellows spends most of his article singing the merits of Federally-subsidized irrigation efforts. Rather the issue that bothered me was that the "facts" of each article did not, put bluntly, agree.

Let's begin with the story I first heard in Fellows' "A Review of the Year 1901," concerning the mountain sheep. To wit:

> Upon one occasion I had the misfortune of falling some twenty feet, but received no serious injury. A mountain sheep was less fortunate, for it was so startled when it saw me that at the first spring it fell off and was killed.

An interesting story, and the writers for *World's Work, Everybody's,* and *The American* took off with it. *World's Work* describes the scene thus:

> Then happened an unusual circumstance. A frightened mountain sheep bounded straight into the arms of Torrence, who grappled the animal with the frenzy of a starving man until Fellows could get his knife. The food crisis was ended.

I didn't recall Fellows mentioning any food crisis, much less that he had butchered the sheep. *Everybody's Magazine* tries to go a little further in the dramatization of the event:

> They had made very little progress because of the hunger within them, and had sunk down at the mouth of

a cleft in the wall to rest, when suddenly a mountain sheep bounded up beside them. Torrence clutched it and hung on like grim death as it tried to escape him. How the sheep got into the cañon and how it had managed to subsist there is a mystery. It was the only living thing the men encountered on their trip, and they ate it in a manner that may not be told, but just as any of us would have eaten it were we dying by inches for want of food.

American Magazine keeps, at least in the telling of this incident, a fairly low profile:

> Provisions were swept away, and if it had not been for the capture of a wounded mountain sheep, their weakness could not have carried them beyond a certain warm cliff side.

Still, two things appeared in these stories that I had no direct evidence for: that Torrence and Fellows suffered some kind of food crisis, seemingly by somehow losing their provisions, and that they ate the sheep to survive. I truly believed that in myth, even cultural myth, there exists some grain of truth, yet I had nothing; had each of these "journalists" built their stories on the half-truths of the previous?

Take the matter of the length of the trip, for example: no one had it quite right. In "Review," and in his journal, Fellows frames the trip from the 12th to the 21st of August, or nine days, which includes his return to Montrose. *Western Farm Life* put the trip at one week; *American Magazine* claimed it took ten days; *World's Work* told of a thirteen-day trip, ten of those in the most difficult part of the canyon; and *Everybody's Magazine* proudly claimed Torrence and Fellows took two weeks to reach the Falls of Sorrow, and then *another* two days to get out.

Many of the articles described what I termed "The Leaps"; specifically, two occasions where the adventurers were supposedly confronted with a natural bridge or falls in the river, and were forced to jump into the water and let it carry them to the other side. This seems unlikely from the outset, and the reports of them don't help the tale's credibility.

American Magazine talks about the two leaps, and each of them go something like this:

> Fellows leaped, and like a pine chip over the top of a mill dam his body flashed for an instant into view and then was gone.

Everybody's Magazine followed suit:

> . . . Twice they let the river's rush carry them through subterranean caverns, blindly trusting to the God that waits on duty.

World's Work heavily dramatized the "event," and added dialogue:

> Suddenly the river presented the phenomenon of a horizon. Here was a fall. The stream reached it between two abutments. Wading cautiously, they tried to round these but there was no hold for feet or hands. They could not gauge the depth nor see what lay beyond.

"What next?" shouted Torrence in Fellows's[sic] ear.

"Over!" responded the senior. "I first!"

The other nodded and the hands met in an eloquent grip.

Two minutes later Fellows disappeared over the fall. Torrence gazed at the spot where his chief had vanished, then plunged after him. Bruised, bleeding, and dazed, he finally gained a crag; nearby, in a similar plight, he saw Mr. Fellows. Looking back at the sixty-foot sheer fall of water, they realized that there could be no turning back.

I liked this one not only because it seemed such pure rubbish, but also because it put a sixty-foot falls in the river. There isn't one, not even close.

What did Fellows have to say about such things? In *Forest and Irrigation*, the man wrote:

Exploration was safely concluded by swimming.

If any of these stories have even the tiniest basis in fact, Fellows proved again his capacity for understatement.

Inconsistencies were everywhere in these articles. On the topic of Torrence's selection as partner, some magazines had him volunteering, while some referred to him as an office aide, which was impossible, since Torrence lived in Montrose and Fellows' office was in Denver. As to the initiation of the project and the inception of the trip itself, there are even more varying and ridiculous accounts.

With all of these, I was bound to have a favorite inconsistency. It came in the form of the descriptions of their slowest day: "Over half a day in making less than a quarter mile";

"Three miles in 24 hours"; "Hours traversing a few rods"; "Three hours covering sixty feet"; "Half a day to win a scant fifty feet."

I decided to see who had them going the slowest. Assuming 14 hour travel days, 16.5 feet to a rod, and so on, I came up with this:

The fastest was in *World's Work*, whose description translated to .125 miles per hour. The slowest came from *American Magazine*, who gave them .001 miles per hour. The winner for most likely accuracy came, oddly enough, in *Everybody's Magazine*, whose result of .034 miles per hour came the closest to Fellows' .036 miles per hour.

It must have been getting late in the day, because I next made a graph showing the date of publication on the "x" axis and the reported slowest speed on the "y" axis. Result? After Fellows' description in 1902, there is a sharp spike in their speed in '07 with *World's Work*, which returns nearly to where it started by '09 and *Everybody's Magazine*, followed by a severe drop in their speed by '11 and a steady but slow increase by the time *Western Farm Life* got to the story in '38.

What did this graph show? Two things; first, I needed to stop researching earlier in the day. Second, I needed better sources of information. I needed more from the people who were there.

That evening, I hit my second brick wall.

8.

IN ONE OF HIS LAST ACTS as President of the United States of America, Herbert Hoover dedicated the Black Canyon of the Gunnison National Monument on March 2nd, 1933, setting aside twelve miles of river and protecting it from development. On October 21st, 1999, it gained the added status of becoming of a National Park. Interestingly, not all of what could be considered Black Canyon lies within the park; there are fifty-three miles between its entrance at Blue Mesa Dam to the canyon's junction with the North Fork of the Gunnison. Over that distance, the Gunnison River falls a little over 2,100 feet, averaging forty-odd feet per mile. Within the Monument, the drop averages considerably more, at around ninety-five feet per mile. This makes it one of the steepest rivers in North America, and definitely the steepest for its size.

It is a remarkably deep canyon; at its westernmost point within the Monument, Black Canyon is nearly 3,000 feet deep. It is also remarkably narrow; in the Narrows, the canyon is 1,725 feet deep, 1,150 feet wide at the top, and forty feet wide at the river. At Painted Wall overlook, the canyon is as deep as it is wide at the rim, 2,300 feet each.

The effects of erosion, and the long job of carving this canyon, began some two million years ago, the culmination of a preparatory process that began to fall into place sixty million years previous. The river ran over ancient and rising rocks, carrying silt from upstream that acted like sandpaper and gradually, immeasurably, it began to wear away a slit, a trench, and ultimately a gorge. The walls were attacked by rain, entering small cracks and freezing in winter, getting trapped within the stone; as the water froze it expanded, prying the rock apart like a ratchet, making a larger crack for the next year's rain, the next year's freeze. The process went on, year after year, and still goes on today, a bit more slowly because of the three upstream dams.

But it is the highest conceit to think that we humans have slowed the process in any measurable way. This canyon was carved in the early Pleistocene, and has been cut at a rate of one foot every thousand years; to imagine that the canyon will not continue on with its next foot of depth in this millennium is absurd. Even if the dams that were built upstream last a thousand years, two thousand, even ten thousand years, their eventual withering will aid in the river's effort to make up for lost time; after all, ten thousand years of impeded work amounts to a mere ten feet in three thousand. Before Blue Mesa, Morrow Point, and Crystal Dams, the Gunnison could, during its floodstage, run at nearly 20,000 cubic feet per second. This translates into roughly 4.5 *million* horsepower generated through the fifty miles of canyon. The dams have leveled out the flow of water, allowing a degree of control; but we cannot control it forever.

In the meantime, the dams have the same types of effects here as they do elsewhere in the world (such as on the Colorado or Columbia Rivers). Erosion is temporarily reduced, sediment is trapped behind the dams. Lacking floods to scour the bottom, the canyon tends to collect more debris than it used to. The temperature of the river drops, since it is fed from the cold bottom of the reservoir behind the dam, and this upsets and often eliminates a few native plants, fish, insects, birds, or their correlative dependents on up the food chain. Some of these changes are irreparable, and the losses they represent should be mourned. But some of the indigenous species will survive until the dams erode into talus indistinguishable from the natural rock. Fear not; the word for "dam" is at most 600 years old, a little over seven inches in Black Canyon time. This too, will pass.

What has made it through these affronts? What flora and fauna abound? As far as plants, only the kind a desert rat could love. At the rim exist prickly pear cactus, a delicacy, when well prepared; scrub oak, seemingly designed to impede travel; and the ferocious yucca, with its sharp bayonette-styled leaves waiting to run your shin through. The service-berry bush makes its home here, where Utes used to employ it in the process of pemmican-making, arrow-making, and doubtless hundreds of other endeavors. A smattering of wildflowers and herbs, the odd mahogany bush, and twisted junipers and piñon pines round out the rim. In the depths live mountain maples, chokebrush, willow, and nearly endless varieties of poison ivy.

Animals? Most of the animals mentioned in guide books are so shy as to make one wonder if they haven't given up and moved on. But the list seems impressive: raccoons, deer, chipmunks, ground squirrels, weasels, badgers, marmots, coyotes, porcupines, elk, black bear, bobcats, cougars, and on occasion humans make up the ground-dwelling mammals. In the air, the list includes golden and bald eagles, nuthatches, owls, hawks, swifts, swallows, turkey vultures, the endangered peregrine falcon, and the bat, my personal favorite. Add this to any number of insects both graceful and creepy and you have the makings for a spectacular ecosystem, even when you take into account the species that just aren't here any more. Things need to share space, after all; two hundred years ago there weren't any people near the canyon. Perhaps when we arrived the big-horned mountain sheep decided to clear out in deference to our personal space.

After only five miles of paved road from the highway, one reaches the border of the park at the South Rim. The visitor center at Gunnison Point attracts some 1,500 people each day, and that number is on the rise. There are two campgrounds, one on each rim, and each site has its own charcoal grill and picnic table. On the South Rim there are a number of very short trails that all, more or less, reach the edge of the canyon, allowing numerous opportunities for those inclined to waste film in a vain effort to capture the depths for all eternity.

Even at half a million visitors per year, the Black Canyon manages to retain its primitive nature. How? By not building trails to the canyon floor. There are nearly a dozen marked "routes" to the river from both rims, but none of them are, by any definition, maintained trails. These routes are for the hardy, they are for the adventurous; in short, they are a pain in the ass. If you carry anything, it takes all day to get down, most of another day to get up, there's no running water at the bottom other than the Gunnison, and for most people it's really just as nice from the top.

Are they planning trails? It doesn't seem like it. A mini-pamphlet I received explained the recently increased entrance fees, that the new fees will be used for "complete replacement of the South Rim Visitor Center at Gunnison Point with the new Discovery Center," and to "provide new exhibits inside the new Discovery Center." Obviously the Department of the Interior knows who most of its paying visitors are, and the whole arrangement is fine by me. Raze the rim, guard the gorge. I'm all for it.

But I know some people might think otherwise. The mandate, and conundrum, that faces the National Park Service each and every morning is to manage, and a dichotomous Act of Congress in 1916 doesn't make it easy: "The Service thus established shall promote and regulate the use of the federal areas known as national parks, monuments, and reservations . . . which purpose is to conserve the scenery and the natural and historic objects and the wildlife therein and to provide for the enjoyment of the same in such manner and by such means as will leave them unimpaired for the enjoyment of future generations."

The NPS is asked to preserve and "provide for the enjoyment" of the parks under their care, not an easy task in an era of budget constraints. Doubtless at some point the same people who thought it was a good idea to allow fee-paying tour operator helicopters to fly into the Grand Canyon will advise a wheelchair-accessible toll ramp be built from South Rim Drive to the Gunnison River. Will this provide for the enjoyment of future generations? I don't know, and no one has asked me; nevertheless, I hold serious reservations about the prospect of Black Canyon 'improvement'.

The Grand Canyon was set aside because one man, who happened to be President, saw it and thought every American should see it, too. Should every American see the Black Canyon? Perhaps; but I don't think every American needs to go to the bottom. The same people who see the Louvre in a single day should have the opportunity to drive on the South Rim, hop out once or twice, or not at all, and get back to their hotel that evening, safely out of the park doing as little harm as possible. As Americans, one of our inalienable rights should be to give our national treasures no more than a cursory glance, if that's all we want.

Another right should be to be allowed, if we so choose, to risk our collective necks sliding and crashing our way to the bottom, to see the canyon as those before us did. To that end I must give credit where it is due, specifically to the Ranger who grants a backcountry permit to the cocky, ill-informed adventurer, and with words of warning and a slow shake of his head allows for enjoyment in the manner of past generations. To these men and women I give thanks, and suggest they keep up the noble work of humbling the nation.

1.

THE MAN HAD HIS HAND ON HIS GUN as he spoke, and I remember feeling a little bit nervous.

At my wife's suggestion, I began going over bibliographies of books I had initially read for my article research. More than one quoted a Dr. Beidleman, who wrote a series of papers on the history of the Black Canyon some years ago. Thinking he might be an untapped expert, I began searching for his work.

After an exhaustive session on the inter-library computer system, I came across an unpublished paper titled "Exploration of the Black Canyon," apparently part of a series Beidleman had written. This paper was at the public library in Montrose, was listed as an "historical document," and in fact was just a photocopy of the manuscript text. Nevertheless, after I had spoken with a librarian over the phone, she agreed to send me a copy of the work through the mail.

Three days later it arrived, and I read through it. At first I was disappointed; much of Beidleman's account of the Fellows/Torrence trip seemed to be lifted directly from the pages of what I felt to be the least reliable articles of the time (*World's Work, Everybody's Magazine,* etc.). Suspicion had become my working philosophy.

But there were a few things Beidleman mentioned that interested me. The first was that he claimed an actual point where Fellows and Torrence had left the Canyon:

> Two days later they encountered an inviting side canyon, opposite the mouth of Smith's Fork, northwest of the present western boundary of the Monument, and decided to forsake the river. . . . scrambled 2000 feet up the Devil's Slide, then hiked fourteen miles to the ranchhouse of the MacMillans back of the rim, guided by a light in a window. The MacMillans gave them a hearty meal, bundled them into a wagon, and that night drove them to Hotchkiss and on to Delta. There they boarded the train to Montrose, where a crowd of 300 people had gathered at the station to greet them.

I wondered where Beidleman got his information. I consulted my map of the area, and found Smith's Fork right where it was supposed to be, but saw nothing marked as the Devil's Slide (although it might not have been significant enough for my map or, arguably, nearly any ascent from the Canyon would be worthy of such a name).

The other thing Beidleman had to say that grabbed my attention was this:

> Most of the equipment had been lost or abandoned in the river chasm, but among things saved was Fellows'

black, cloth-bound engineering record book containing valuable records which would facilitate the future construction of a water diversion tunnel.

I immediately flipped to Beidleman's bibliography, hoping to find mention of this book. It wasn't there. I jumped on the phone to Paul at the Black Canyon, and asked him about Beidleman. He said he had never met him, but a few people who worked there had, and said nothing but good things about him. He gave me Beidleman's address, and I slammed out a quick letter to him, begging him for his sources.

In the meantime, I looked at other things in the bibliography. Among the texts I recognized was a booklet by Barton Marsh, "The Uncompahgre Valley and the Gunnison Tunnel, Special Tunnel Opening Edition" from 1909. I found it in the archives downtown, again puzzled by its not showing up on earlier searches.

The book had little new to tell me, but there was one photo that stopped me dead. It was clearly taken in the bottom of the canyon, the face I recognized clearly as Torrence, and he was clearly holding a dead sheep in his hands. Was there more to this sheep thing than I had thought? Maybe so, although this truly proved nothing more than that a sheep had died, perhaps exactly as Fellows described in "Review."

That little mystery would have to wait; I had other leads to follow. Beidleman's bibliography mentioned a report to the U.S. Geological Survey, and for that I had to head to the Denver Federal Center, west of town.

Which is where I was confronted by the armed man. As I approached the gate into the Center, I rolled down my window and put on a smile. The man who came up to me wasn't wearing one; neither, I noticed, was his partner, also armed, who approached the other side of my car with caution. I rolled down that window too, as a sign of goodwill.

"Where are you going?" asked the first. He was a little brusque, I thought, but I remembered that the trials were still going on for the Oklahoma City Federal Building bombing suspects in Denver, and I imagined no one here had been quite themselves lately.

"I'm heading for, uh, Building 22," I answered. "The U.S.G.S."

He regarded me briefly. His partner said, "What're you doing there?"

I quickly fumbled for my note pad, spilling several three-by-five cards onto the floor. I showed him the numbers for the report I was looking for, stammered something about the Black Canyon and dead hydrologists, and forked over my driver's license and social security card.

The nutty professor act worked, and they waved me through. Five feet inside the Center, I slammed on the brakes and backed up. Both guards ran up to me.

"One more thing," I said sheepishly. "Where is it?"

This time I got a smile, and a map.

10.

THE UNITED STATES GEOLOGICAL SURVEY building was small, unassuming, surrounded by federally expelled smokers, and inside smelled a lot like meatloaf. This last I attributed to the cafeteria on the first floor.

The guard at the front entrance directed me to the library on the second floor, where I found the nice woman I had spoken to on the phone about the survey report. She didn't have exactly what I asked for, but she thought it was the only thing vaguely like it in the building. She handed me a little green book entitled "First Reclamation Service Conference Report, 1901," and showed me a flagged article by I. W. McConnell, resident engineer, called "Topographic Work in the Grand Canyon of the Gunnison." I thumbed through it; it contained a few vague references to Fellows, one to Torrence, and just a hint of the expedition (I should have expected as much from an engineer by now):

> In 1901 Mr. A. L. Fellows, now district engineer, U. S. Geological Survey, Denver, Colo., taking a single companion,

> Mr. William W. Torrence . . . made an exploring trip from Cimarron to Red Rock Canyon. This trip, made under great difficulty and involving prodigious labor on the part of the explorers, covered practically all that part of the canyon not traversed by the Denver and Rio Grande Railway.

Cimarron was universally identified as the starting point for the expedition; but Red Rock Canyon was inside the present park, miles upstream of Smith's Fork, where Beidleman thought they came out. I had noted Red Rock on my map earlier, even before my own trip to the canyon, as a possible place to come out. Obviously my wife and I didn't make it that far; but had Torrence and Fellows? Or had they gone further, to the "inviting" side canyon near Smith's?

Flipping back a few pages, there was an article by Fellows himself, called "Projects Considered," where he outlined a few reclamation ideas the engineers had been mulling over, mentioned the tunnel project, and briefly explained why he kept his office in Denver: it was centrally located to all the Colorado projects under consideration. He neglected to mention his trip, perhaps preferring to let others blow his horn for him.

I photocopied the articles, returned the book, and asked the librarian if there was any way of finding out whether they had other papers by Fellows. She smiled broadly and led me to a line of expensive-looking computer terminals, asking who I was looking for.

"Fellows," I said.

"First initials?" she asked. "Or do you know the full name?"

"A. L.," I replied, and with a grin added, "Abraham Lincoln."

This always got a smile from librarians. As soon as I mentioned that he had been the first to go down a canyon, she started laughing knowingly and talking about "river-runners," and how she "gets a lot of that here." I started to explain that, in fact, most of his time had likely been spent walking, but by then she had found another citation. It was over in the Bureau of Reclamation building, halfway across the center. She printed me out a listing, and wished me luck.

After becoming lost and asking twice, I found the building; it turned out to be one I had circled several times and eliminated. I entered the front door, and was given a visitor badge after signing in. This was new, and I felt rather foolish, but I wore it and headed for the Bureau's library.

Inside I was greeted by a wonderfully prim woman who was everything I could have wished for in a librarian; she was direct, seemed a little bit in a hurry, and hated computers. I loved her instantly, and as we started flipping through listings together, I felt I had discovered someone who simply adored her job, and wouldn't trade it for anything.

It took nearly half an hour to discover that the papers I wanted had been moved to the National Archives building which, fortuitously enough, was also inside the Federal Center. I hoped the security men weren't keeping tabs on me, as I had left my flight plan hours ago. This time I decided to walk, as it was just a building or two over.

I found it quickly, thanks to the huge sign in front which read "Records of the National Archives—Rocky Mountain Region." They were also remodeling, and I quickly found more people who loved their jobs and loved visitors nearly as much. One particularly nice woman checked me in, had me sign a few papers, and presented me with an I.D. card, good for two years, that identified me as a federally-approved and qualified researcher. It had my name, a few numbers, the seal of the National Archives and Records Administration, and the signature of the woman who had taken me under her wing, Joan.

She tried to explain how to look for something, and I explained what I was looking for. I didn't understand much of what she was saying, but fortunately she understood me, and retrieved seven boxes of papers, set me up at a desk, and left me to dig in.

In the tradition of the best Mormon settlers, it seemed the government never threw any kind of paper record away. I spent hours sifting through the boxes, looking at letters, reports, bills, and engineering sketches. I found the incredibly long report Fellows filed in 1904 about the prospects for the tunnel, and got a photocopy of a quite detailed topographical map that had been drawn showing the initial site for the diversion dam. They had chosen the Narrows, where the canyon is only forty feet wide at the river; its inaccessibility eventually led to moving the site upstream.

From the letters back and forth, I discovered that Fellows had been a driving force behind the formation of the Uncompahgre Valley Water User's Association, a local group whose existence and apparent enthusiasm for the tunnel project had been pivotal in the Federal Government's eventual approval and fund appropriation. It also seemed that Fellows was briefly taken off, or at least distanced from the project itself, a matter that annoyed him greatly. Eventually he was reassigned to help lead the project, but the temporary betrayal may have permanently soured him on the project.

At any rate, hours later I emerged from the Archives, carrying only a photocopy of the map and of a photograph included in Fellows' report, captioned in his distinctive scrawl "Gunnison Cañon at Boat Landing, Aug. 20th 1901." I didn't recognize the landscape in the photo enough to know exactly where it was taken, but the rock behind the river sloped away enough to where I thought it was reasonably far down the canyon. This made sense, as Fellows' "dayplanner" had him back in Montrose by the following day.

The light outside had dimmed; it seemed as if a storm were on the way. The radio confirmed my prognosis, and I decided to head home.

II.

THE FIRST BIG SNOWSTORM of the year hit Denver, and I became a shut-in. Which, I suppose, is not a bad thing for a qualified researcher; more time for researching, after all. But sadly, with ten inches of snow on the ground and another eight on the way in the next few hours, there was no hope of visiting any library or archive. I decided to turn up the heat, spread out my ever-growing pile of photocopies, and pore.

One of the few papers I hadn't really looked at in depth had come out of the "Papers," a biographical sketch someone had compiled of old A. Lincoln sometime around 1931. The caption claimed it had been "revised and brought down to date" from a similar sketch done in *Who's Who*, and it broke down something like this:

His name was Abraham Lincoln Fellows. At the time of this sketch, he was Senior Irrigation Engineer within the Division of Irrigation of the Bureau of Agricultural Engineering, part of the U.S. Department of Agriculture, and was 67 years old. He lived at this time at 2406 Dana St., in Berkeley, California.

His birthday was November 1st, 1864. Although I found no evidence that he knew or cared, he was a Scorpio. His parents were the Reverend Franklin Ebenezer and Jane Eliza Fellows.

He attended prep school in Norwich, Connecticut, and went on to earn his B.A. from Yale in 1886. Upon graduation, he became a prep school teacher for a year, then abandoned that course and became a chainman for the Montezuma Valley Irrigation Company. He worked there for ten years, and by 1897 became their chief engineer. According to this sketch, he was also in that time the County Surveyor and Superintendent of Schools.

From 1897 to 1905, Fellows filled any number of positions, and in any possible order. He was Resident Hydrographer for the U.S.G.S., Deputy State Irrigation Engineer for the State of Colorado, and District Engineer for the newly formed U.S. Reclamation Service. I imagined he was all things to all government organizations, and although there was enough documentation to put him at each position at all times, my brain told me that there must have been considerable "flow" in responsibilities and duties in turn-of-the-century Colorado. I decided that attempting to determine exactly when he was at what post would not only be impossible, but unnecessary; suffice it to say he was well considered and relied upon by the powers that were.

The rest of the sketch seemed accurate, and more or less jibed with what I had inferred from previous research. He called it quits with Colorado in 1905, largely due to his being distanced from the Gunnison project. North Dakota offered him a position as State Irrigation Engineer, and he took it and left; December of that same year he married one Blanche Irene McCoy, of Webster, Pennsylvania.

What we know of Blanche largely comes from an unpublished genealogy book written by her daughter, Dorothy Fellows Haines. Blanche attended the school where A. L. was superintendent; seventeen years his junior, she played the piano, painted, and studied to become a kindergarten teacher. They were married on December 20th, 1905 (Blanche was 24, A. L. 41).

As a married man, Fellows managed to stick with the government in North Dakota for only two years, becoming the Secretary and General Manager for Field, Fellows, and Hinderlider Engineering Company of Denver in 1907. This was a great little company and, given the staff, probably made a lot of money. John E. Field (also a Yale alum) was the State Engineer for Colorado from 1897 to 1899. Michael C. Hinderlider came out of Purdue with a civil engineering degree, and went on to be a state hydrographer and a lead engineer for the U.S. Reclamation Service. The firm managed to get several big accounts, including a lot of work for the City of Denver and the American Beet Sugar Company.

This lasted until 1918, during which time Fellows also managed to become a member and twice president of the Denver Public Utilities Commission, the City Engineer for Denver, and a member of the Board of Public Works. The taste for public service thus re-whetted, in 1918 (and until, it seemed, at least 1931) he became the Senior Irrigation Engineer for the U.S. Department of Agriculture.

The next section of the sketch was headed, "notable accomplishments," and I was happy to see included among these his exploration of the Black Canyon in 1901. After that he was credited with "initiating" the Uncompahgre Valley Tunnel Project from 1901-1905. Then the sketch listed things I never expected:

> ... Determining boundaries of National Forests in Colo. as established by executive order of Pres. Theodore Roosevelt, and of Mesa Verde National Park (Colo.) as created by Act of Congress. . . .

At first I thought that perhaps later in life Fellows had become something of a conservationist; odd, I thought, as I had come to think of him as more of a wilderness *conqueror*. Then I realized that this entry in the sketch was probably an overly romantic account of events. After all, he was an engineer; most likely he "determined boundaries" for all kinds of things with theolodite and tripod, wherever he was sent.

The sketch finished off with a few personal notes. He was a member of the American Society of Agricultural Engineers, a Mason, and a Congregationalist. Under the listing of hobbies, the sketch mentioned "hiking." That, as I would come to find out, was putting it mildly.

I also had in my possession a second sketch, taken out of an enormous Colorado History book I had stumbled across in the back of the library. It was considerably longer than the *Who's Who*, and leaned more toward the personal.

It seemed from this "sketch" that Fellows' father (the Rev. Franklin) was a Dartmouth graduate who served as a chaplain in the Civil War. Jane Eliza, the Reverend's wife, was a New York native and something of an aristocrat, counting among her own family members a Yale University President who, if you believe in that sort of thing, might have had a bit to do with A. L.'s decision to study there.

The Reverend Franklin and Jane Eliza Fellows had eight children (of which A. L. was the sixth), five sons and three daughters. Abraham's unquestionably recognizable name came as a result of a rare sort of Congregationalist baptism his father performed, the "baptism for the dead." The Reverend was a huge fan of the late President Abraham Lincoln, but was immensely saddened that he had never undertaken the rite of baptism. To clear the matter posthumously required him to name his son after the President and baptize the pair of them at once, through a kind of biblical surrogacy apparently qualified by the quotation, "Why baptize ye for the dead if Christ be not risen?" This particular sketch went on to explain that this form of baptism is performed "even today" by some members of the Mormon church.

It continued along the lines of the personal with the revelation that Fellows was presented in January of 1905 with a gold watch, "beautifully inscribed," as a token of appreciation from the people of the Uncompahgre Valley for all the work he did with concern to the Uncompahgre Project. It was one of his most highly prized items.

This business with the watch stood out for me. It was given to him the same year he briefly called it quits with Colorado, and at first glance I thought it was some kind of send off, but he was given the watch three months before he left.

I came to appreciate just how highly the people of Montrose thought of A. L. Fellows through a couple of articles in the *Montrose Press*. The first was dated September 18, 1902, a piece where the reporter stumbles up to the rim of the Black Canyon with a few of the key players. Specifically, he travels with the Anderson brothers (August and Eric, the latter of the failed 1900 expedition) and J. E. Pelton himself (leader and financial backer for that same trip) to visit Fellows' surveying camp.

> ... The party strolled along the brink of this great chasm for two or three miles, while Mr. Fellows pointed out the rapids, waterfalls and many other obstacles that he and his party had to contend with while making the survey of the canyon which he has just completed for the tunnel site. One has but to see the many dangers to realize what a Herculean task Mr. Fellows has undertaken and has successfully completed.

The other article was dated March 10, 1905, a report on Fellows' resignation:

> ... Every citizen of the Uncompahgre valley will feel the loss of the presence of Mr. Fellows ... as a distinctly personal one. While others originated the idea of bringing water to this valley by means of a tunnel from the Gunnison river, yet it required the mastermind and indomitable zeal of Mr. Fellows to interest the government in the great enterprise and leave no stone unturned to have the work actually started.
> Late in the fall when large financial interests were using all manner of chicanery to prevent the Taylor-Moore Construction company getting the contract upon the tunnel,

Mr. Fellows plunged into the breach with all his energy. It was his influence in the end that caused the secretary of the interior to finally approve the company's bond so work could actually commenced [sic.].

In the midst of this suspense he remarked to a friend: "For six weeks I have been working day and night and have not had one good night's sleep in all that time. Several hard trips were made to Washington and the strain is telling upon me; but if my strength will hold out I will continue until all obstacles are removed." And he did, for soon thereafter the glad news flashed over the wire that the bond was approved.

As an engineer of great ability, the reputation of Mr. Fellows was fully established when the U. S. Government accepted his recommendations and agreed to undertake the construction of this project as one of the very first under the new reclamation act. Mr. Fellows has reached his present high standing as an engineer by his own efforts— he has climbed the ladder of fame because he possessed the brain, body, and energy. He commenced on the lowest rung a poor but honest boy. The position he has attained, not only in the professional world, but in the hearts of men, will remain so long as there lives one to tell the story.

That last would be me, I suppose.

The people loved him, or at least the newspaper editor did. The bit about Fellows starting out as a "poor but honest boy" should probably be put alongside the one about George Washington and the doomed apple tree; but there is another story in this farewell column that deserves more attention.

It has to do with the Taylor-Moore Construction Company.

INTERLUDE 1.

On September 23rd, 1909, the Gunnison Tunnel was officially opened. This marked the appreciable end of an appreciably long and convoluted story. There was an enormous celebration; after all, this was the largest man-made tunnel in the world. The tunnel was 5.8 miles long, eleven feet wide, twelve feet high, running from one of the most inaccessible points in America through one of the hardest chunks of stone in the world. It could carry over a thousand cubic feet of water every second to an otherwise dry valley, increasing land values tenfold. The city government at Montrose paid to bring President Taft out to this tiny town to ceremoniously open the gates.

Flanked by a militia formed of armed sheriffs representing every county in the state, Taft made his way to a raised podium where, after a brief speech, he touched a specially-made gold bell to a silver plate, signaling to open the headgates.

But the planners of this great to-do faced a minor logistical problem. The distance from the Gunnison River to the town's little platform was nearly six miles, and water would take upwards of half an hour to cover it. Even before the onset of the Television Age, this kind of delay was more than observers would endure. Accordingly, an alternate plan was developed.

What actually happened was when Taft touched the bell to the plate, a signal went down a wire to a small group of workers hidden just inside the tunnel. They had spent the day previous erecting a temporary wooden dam, which had collected seep water from porous sections of the rock. When they got the signal, they took sledge hammers to their creation and, minutes later, a small trickle of water made its way laboriously to the site of the revelers. The crowd reportedly cheered for a full five minutes.

There were a number of letters written back and forth at the onset of the Tunnel's construction, and while I simply glanced over them at the National Archives, Paul had taken the time to photocopy them, find something interesting, and send them on to me.

The story they told went something like this.

The Uncompahgre Project (the Gunnison Tunnel) was approved by the Reclamation Service on March 14, 1903. By this time the nature, location, and length of the tunnel and resultant canal system had been pretty much determined, and all there was left to do was actually build the thing.

The Reclamation Service naturally sought bids from private contractors to do the job, and after they advertised on July 29, 1904, they received a number of competing bids. This happens, I am told, on every government contract.

But there was something about these bids that didn't make sense to one man, currently holding the position of District Engineer for the U.S.G.S. His name was A. L. Fellows.

Two letters went out from the field to headquarters on October 5, 1904. The first was signed by Fellows and three other engineers, specifically W.H. Sanders, J.H. Quinton, and George Y. Wisner, and was addressed to Frederick Haynes Newell, the Chief Engineer for the U.S.G.S. What this first letter had to say was something of a formality; it basically informed the Chief that there were bids received and outlined what they were. The letter also contained a recommendation on which company to go with; not surprisingly, they recommended the one with the lowest bid, and if anything were to go wrong with them, then the next lowest.

So far so good.

The other letter, however, was of a less formal nature, hand-written for Newell by George Y. Wisner, at that time a consulting engineer in the field. It hinted at something that was not altogether clean:

Dear Sir,

I wish to call your attention to some features of the bids obtained here today for the construction of the Gunnison Tunnel which could not properly be mentioned in our official report.

You will note from the abstract of bids accompanying our report that the bid of the Taylor-Moore construction company was $414,450 less than the next bid.

This lowest bid is not far from what the work can be done for without contingencies or profits, and I am afraid that an effort will be made to have them fail to qualify.

The next two bids are sufficiently large to give the contractors a good profit—without the bonus of $60,000 [an early completion bonus] or the forfeit of $60,000 [a late completion penalty] . . . .

I think that the Taylor-Moore company *were the only bidders* who submitted a bid on the basis of obtaining the $60,000 [i.e., planning on finishing on-time or ahead of schedule], and I therefore wish to emphasize the request of the Board that in case the lowest bidder qualifies, the Department give them the benefit of all the time possible by having the contract executed without delay . . . .

Sincerely yours,

Geo. Y. Wisner

In my opinion, what had happened was that Fellows noticed that the other companies who submitted a bid had all devised their figures based on not finishing the project on time. He pointed it out to Wisner, and I suspect had Wisner write the letter because he feared his own objectivity might be questioned, since he had been involved so intimately with the project for so long. To his credit, he managed to keep his own mouth shut for a full day.

On October 6, 1904, Fellows sent this letter to Newell.

Sir:

I desire to call your attention particularly to certain features connected with the bids forwarded to you by yesterday's registered mail. . . .

It will be noted that there is a very wide divergence in the bids, the lowest bidders, the Taylor-Moore Construction Co., being $413,550 less than any other bidder. Knowing the Taylor Moore construction co. to be perfectly well informed as to what they were doing, Mr. Taylor and his assistants having made a thorough study of the situation . . . and moreover, these estimates agree almost exactly with the estimates contained in my report submitted to you last Spring, I am firmly of the opinion that the bid should be accepted. . . . I am satisfied that they were the only bidders who did not add $120,000 to their estimates in the belief that they would lose both the bonus and be compelled to pay the penalty.

It would certainly be the height of injustice for the government to induce any bidder to depend upon receiving a bonus through rapid work and then to hamper him by delaying him unnecessarily at the commencement of his work. I strongly urge that the contracts be made out and signed at the earliest possible moment, and that the successful bidders be notified by wire. . . . I do not believe that the Service can in justice do less than make the time between the receipt of the bids and the official acceptance of same as short as possible.

Once again, so far so good. Everyone recommends that the government go with the lowest, and seemingly most knowledgeable, bidder.

But by the 25th, things had changed. The nature of the different companies was made clear to Fellows; specifically, that the bids that all hovered together at nearly half a million dollars high were from Colorado companies.

Taylor-Moore was based out of Texas.

On October 25, Fellows circulated a long memorandum among the consulting board members locally, then copied it and sent it along to Newell the next day.

Gentlemen:

The report [we sent to Newell] . . . recommended that the contract be awarded to the Taylor-Moore Construction Company of Hillsboro, Tex., and in case of any default . . . that the contract be awarded to Lusk & McClurg [the next lowest bidders], 46 Railroad Building, Denver, Colo., with the additional statement that "we consider either of the three lowest bidders reasonable."

. . . The Taylor-Moore company was notified by wire upon October 18, 1904 that the award was made to it, and contracts were sent upon the same day for signature. This being but seven days since, and at last accounts the contracts not having been received by the Taylor-Moore Construction Co., it is too early to state positively whether or not said company will qualify, but the following statements are known to be facts beyond reasonable doubt:

The Taylor-Moore Construction Company, even before the awarding of the contract, was endeavoring in good faith to secure a surety bond [necessary before taking on a government contract] from some responsible surety company, but it has met with unexpected difficulties.

It may have nothing to do with the case, but it is a fact that one of the members of the firm which is the next lowest firm of bidders [Lusk & McClurg] is closely allied with the monied interests of the country, being, in fact, the son-in-law of one of the principal bankers and capitalists of the United States. Whether this has anything to do with the case or not, it seems a fact that the surety companies have been warned that they should have nothing to do with the proposed bond, unless collateral to the full amount of the bond is placed in the hands of the surety company signing the bond, and a very large premium is demanded in addition.

The terms then are apparently almost intolerable, and owing to the fact that nearly all the surety companies have formed a combination, it would be an easy matter for them to prevent the said Taylor-Moore Construction Company from getting a surety bond under anything like tolerable conditions.

. . . The contingency of the Construction Company being unable to give a satisfactory bond owing to the forming of a combination against them, should be guarded against.

Fellows goes on to suggest that it would be better to accept the calculated risk of allowing Taylor-Moore to submit with a personal (rather than corporate) bond, instead of allowing the government to lose that half a million dollars it would cost with the next lowest bidder. He also mentions his opinion of the validity of their estimates on cost (because they so closely match his), and on their capacity to do the job. They employ "the very best tunnel men in the State, and perhaps in the country." He goes on:

> In view of these facts it appears to me that it would be criminal on the part of the Reclamation Service to permit the people of the Uncompahgre Valley to be robbed of half a million dollars in order that some of the men of the capitalist class should reap a tremendous profit.

Then he suggests a drastic measure to prevent that from happening:

> In case the Taylor-Moore Construction Company fails to qualify, the Reclamation Service do neither let the contract to the next lowest bidder, nor readvertise, but proceed to construct the Gunnison tunnel *directly, under the direction of the Government engineers.*

Fellows signed this letter, tacked it to another stating pretty much the same thing, and sent it all to Newell in Washington.

On the 27th, Fellows received a letter from James Taylor of Taylor-Moore, stating that he has been thwarted at every turn, but can get an individual bond from a rich friend in Galveston if he can have until November 21st to secure the deal.

On the 28th, Wisner gets back into the game by writing a letter to Newell stating he does not agree with Fellows that "the Surety Companies of the United States can be controlled by one contracting firm." He thinks Fellows is being alarmist, and that the contract should go to Lusk & McClurg if Taylor-Moore can't qualify.

Newell wrote back on the 31st, with a rather collusive note that remarked that Fellows " . . . has gone off on a tangent; in fact, his letters recently do not seem to indicate cool judgment."

Everyone believes Fellows and Taylor-Moore are out of their minds; that there could be some kind of hidden conspiracy out to get rid of the Texan construction interest in Colorado seemed absurd.

But only until November 28th, when the following letter arrived on Newell's desk, straight from the House of Representatives, signed by Rep. Franklin E. Brooks, of Colorado:

> My dear Mr. Newell:
>
> I understand that the Government contemplates letting the Uncompahgre-Gunnison tunnel contract to a Texas firm of contractors.
>
> I am advised by several people that the bid for this work is below the possibility of its completion, and much doubt is cast upon the practical experience and financial ability of the successful bidders.
>
> There are several firms of Colorado contractors who are interested in this matter, and on their behalf and also on behalf of the state and for the good of the service I very respectfully request that the department make such investigation as it deems fit in view of the statements which have

been made to the end that the work may not be hampered by failure of the contractors.

Very truly yours,

Franklin E. Brooks

Something about this letter raised Newell's hackles, and he started taking Fellows seriously. By November 18th, he had a letter off to A. F. Davis, Assistant Chief Engineer, letting him know that he had asked Fellows to go to Washington to confer with him about the tunnel. In the letter he also withdraws his first recommendation to accept the next lowest bid, and sides with Fellows, thinking that the government should take over the project.

Newell gained a new reason to side with the embattled Taylor-Moore, thanks to a letter he received from James Taylor on the 21st. Taylor tells such a remarkable tale, it would be unfair not to include it here in its entirety:

Dear Sir:

As you are aware the undersigned, constituting the Taylor-Moore Construction Company were awarded the contract for the construction of the Gunnison Tunnel in Colorado; but thus far we have been unable to furnish the required bond.

We beg to call your attention to some of the facts in connection with our failure, up to the present time, to qualify, which will explain the situation, in part at least:

After deciding to estimate on the work, we consulted the General Agent of the National Security Company of New York City, located at Dallas, Texas. At the meeting, the Agent agreed to make our bond without indemnity or collateral. I at once proceeded to Colorado, to investigate the existing conditions to be encountered during the process of construction of said Gunnison Tunnel, and further to investigate the cost of other tunnels of about the same section, and of about the same formation of rock, as the Gunnison Tunnel project.

I was aided in my work by the Leyner Engineering Works, Co., and also by Mr. S.A. Knowles, a tunnel foreman, and contractor of very great experience, and Superintendent of the Newhouse Tunnel at Idaho Springs.

Through Mr. Knowles, I had access to the books and cost of work of the Newhouse Tunnel Company, dating back some five years.

The Newhouse Tunnel has been driven 14500 feet through the hardest granite, and the Superintendent, Mr. Knowles holds the record for feet driven per day, in the State of Colorado.

With the above facts and data before me I felt reasonably safe in basing our estimate upon the costs per lineal foot of the Newhouse Tunnel Company.

The result of the bidding is well known to you. The great difference between our and the next higher bids has been largely the cause of our failure to furnish bonds, the Surety Company demanding at first $150,000 collateral.

After going to the expense of taking the President of the National Surety Co., to Colorado to investigate the situation in person, he modified his demands to one of Indemnity Signers, and himself drew the 14 Indemnity Bond forms and stated he would accept the same in amounts of from $5000 up. We hereupon proceeded to have the bonds executed and wired the said President on the third of November, that we had the indemnity required.

He wires us to come to New York City, which we did, arriving at 3 o'clock p.m. on the 11th, and meeting the gentleman at 8 o'clock, p.m. After going over the indemnity bonds, he stated he could not accept same in such small sums, and therefore could not execute our bond. In reply to the query, as to why he had brought us to New York City, he simply stated that he must have the indemnity bond signed by four people, each worth from at least $250,000 up.

This was, of course, prohibitory, and we feel absolutely confident that this same Surety Company had no intention of executing our bond and only desired to cause us delay, and that on the other hand it was working in collusion with the second bidder.

The strongest influence has been brought to bear upon the Bonding Companies, and financial institutions generally, by the second bidder, Lusk & McClurg.

Bonding Companies and Financial Institutions have been warned that our bid was extremely dangerous, and any company signing our bond would unquestionably lose the amount of the bond.

They [Lusk & McClurg] stated to the President of the Bonding Company, that we could not complete the contract at our figures.

In addition to this they have approached two of the members of our Company with reference to defaulting on our bond.

In view of the above combination of facts, we have thus far failed to make our bond, and now offer for your consideration the very best thing we can do at this time:

We will furnish a personal bond to the extent of $100,000 and will agree to leave in the hands of the Government our certified check of $10,000 and at the end of six months we will furnish the additional amount of a satisfactory $50,000 bond, upon furnishing which our check is to be returned. Failing to furnish the $50,000 bond we will agree that the Government may retain from our monthly estimate $5,000 per month, until the $40,000 has been reached . . . .

I am proceeding to secure the $100,000 bond and expect to reach Washington with same on the morning of the 28th, if not advised to the contrary.

I assure you we regret to the fullest extent the trouble we are putting the Department to. We can not express to you in words our gratitude for the leniency so far shown toward us, and we trust you may find some way to permit us to proceed with the contract, thereby saving the Government and the people the vast sum of $410,000 and making a handsome profit ourselves, which we still feel positive we can do.

Yours very truly,
James T. Taylor

Moved by the letter, Newell started using all of his influence to speed things along for Taylor-Moore. Naturally, such noble action was not to go unchallenged. On the 26th, Davis sent a letter to Newell advising him that Lusk & McClurg had filed an official protest against execution of the contract with Taylor-Moore, and that the House of Representatives had been in constant contact with his office.

For the next several months, however, letters of support from within the department continued to fly, and ultimately the contract was secured for the Taylor-Moore construction company, under a complex web of personal and company-sponsored bonds. But by January, a number of Taylor-Moore's preexisting loans were suddenly recalled under suspicious circumstances, and the company was forced to declare bankruptcy. To its credit, the U.S.G.S. and the Reclamation Service made good on their threats and proceeded to build the Tunnel themselves, hiring local day labor and many of the principal players from Taylor-Moore to get the job done. In the end, none of the influence exerted by the Colorado companies had the desired effect; ultimately no one got the contract.

And as to the popular notion of victors writing history, I offer this quote from the Montrose Centennial Celebration history text:

> In October [1904] the bids were opened for construction of the tunnel, canals, a mountain road to the east portal, and a telephone line. Taylor-Moore Construction Company won the contract, but because of improper equipment and lack of capital was bankrupt within four months. Construction was then supervised by the Reclamation Service.

To paraphrase Napoleon, history is only the version of events we have decided to agree upon.

12.

IT HAD NEVER OCCURRED TO ME, in the course of researching Fellows' story, that I might fail to come across his account of the trip. I had a number of promising leads, evidence, and hearsay that this account existed, and above all a sense that Fellows must have written it all down somewhere. But I really had no guarantee of finding it; some nights I wondered if it would be months or years before I could track it down.

I shouldn't have worried; fate found it for me.

I had come to rely greatly upon the odd fruits of Zen research as a means of bolstering my spirit. One afternoon I found myself downtown at the library, once again "channel-surfing" on the computerized card catalog. Once again, I typed in "Fellows," and initiated a search.

And once again, something new came up.

I asked a librarian about this, about running identical searches and coming up with new listings, and he was baffled. I imagined that my previous searches had loosened the system up, eliminating some kind of digital clog in the Fellows pipe. I knew this was nonsense, but I couldn't explain it sensibly.

The new listing was for a book Fellows had written about the nation's water resources, and it was in a section of the library called the Colorado History Archive. This was a portion of the archives that was open to browsing, and exclusively contained books and pamphlets about the state's history. I dropped off my notebooks and once more braved the metal detectors, finding the book in under a minute.

I flipped to the title page, and checked the date: 1900. It preceded the Black Canyon trip by almost exactly a year, and was perhaps the most boring book I had ever read. It was crammed with numbers and engineering jargon; obviously, it was not intended for the general public. And, since it lacked a bibliography or an author's bio, it was of no use to me in my search. So I put it back on the shelf.

For reasons unclear to me even now, I pulled out the book next to it. It was called "A History of Agriculture in Colorado," by one Alvin T. Steinel. I can't recall why I found it the least bit interesting. The subtitle was "A Chronological Record of Progress in the Development of General Farming, Livestock Production, and Agricultural Education and Investigation, on the Western Border of the Great Plains and in the Mountains of Colorado, 1858 to 1926." It was published in 1926, "in Honor of the Fiftieth Anniversary of the Admission of Colorado to the Union." I couldn't imagine a better anniversary present.

I flipped to the end, finding that most elusive of animals in historical texts: the index. In the "F" section, I found my man Fellows. And on page 530, I found his account of the trip down the Black Canyon, reproduced faithfully by an Agricultural Historian. To quote the good Mr. Steinel, "Fellows' own

story of the exploration will serve the purposes of history."
And it did. And it will. Here is Fellows' introduction:

EXPLORATION OF THE CANON

It was my good fortune to have charge of the government hydrographic work in the State of Colorado at that time and the general direction of the survey, which was made in the summer of 1901, was turned over to me. From the very commencement of the survey I felt it would be necessary before its conclusion to make an exploration in detail of the Grand Canon of the Gunnison which was generally supposed to be impassable. Other parties had tried in vain to explore the gloomy recesses of the canon. Efforts had been made in the winter time to pass through on the ice, but had failed on account of the existence of falls and rapids where no ice could form and these expeditions had been given up. Surveying parties had attempted to go through it with complete outfits but had failed and had given up the efforts after losing their equipment and had painfully worked their way out over the rim of the canon before the most inaccessible points had been reached. In the year 1900, a party of five residents of the Uncompahgre Valley, under the leadership of John E. Pelton of Montrose, had made the best planned and boldest attempt yet undertaken to force their way through the gloomy passages, but after traversing about half the distance, that is to say about twenty miles out of a total of about forty, and after losing one boat and a large part of their supplies, they were forced to abandon their remaining boat and return to their homes by a most toilsome and perilous detour of more than a hundred miles. The veteran old trapper and hunter of that region, Moccasin Bill, offered the encouraging ultimatum that it was impossible for mortal man to go through the canon and live, that he himself had been about half way through and knew no man could go farther.

It was under these far from encouraging conditions and with the prophecy heard from all sources that I would be killed if I undertook the trip, that I made up my mind to at least make the effort.

—A. Lincoln Fellows, 1901

As soon as I read the intro, I also made up my mind to, at least, make the effort. I decided to follow Fellows and Torrence into the canyon.

**13,**

In the meantime, during the two months of surveying, I had never lost an opportunity to study the canon from the top and of finding ways of getting down into it.

—A. Lincoln Fellows, 1901

THE BRIGHT SUN MADE ME SQUINT even behind dark glasses, and the glare from the recent snowfall blinded me further. As I slammed the door on the truck and stood outside, I heard nothing at all; every sound was muffled by the snow. I tied on my boots, bundled up, put on my day pack and prepared to enjoy the off-season. It seemed that, at least for the moment, I had the entire Black Canyon of the Gunnison National Monument to myself.

And that wasn't far from the truth. It was mid-November, and a reasonably large storm had just passed by this part of the state, leaving a foot or so of fresh snow in its wake. That, combined with the renovation (and subsequent temporary closure) of the visitor center made for a mighty empty Monument. That suited me fine; it gave me a chance to look down from all the overlooks I had ignored before, uninterrupted by tourists.

I had seen no other cars that day once I turned off the main highway and headed up Highway 347 towards the park. Although the roads were clear, the cold had its own effects;

not only did it keep visitors away, but I also didn't see any birds fluttering around. I took the pull-off for the first overlook and grabbed a map from a small box. Odd as it sounds, behind the maps was a stack of blank backcountry permits; I couldn't imagine anyone wanting to risk the treacherous canyon walls with so much slippery snow everywhere, much less where they might leave the permit when, or if, they climbed back out.

At any rate, I knew what I had come to see. First, I wanted to get a look at the schist and gneiss walls with a thin coat of snow; second, I wanted to try to see the river. I hadn't explored most of the overlooks on my last visit, and I wondered how many of them had a straight line of sight to the Gunnison. I drove until I came to a sign marking Chasm View, and left the truck to take the short trail to the rim.

The sun had started to melt the snow, and it made a sound like stretching leather under my boots as I walked. It blanketed the open ground, and clung in peach-sized balls to the tips of scrub-oak branches, like some improbable winter fruit. On the path in front of me, I saw only two sets of human tracks, the same person going in and coming out. The prints had the thick heel and purposeful stride of a ranger's boot, and were flanked on either side by rabbit tracks. The spacing seemed to indicate that the ranger had spooked one rabbit into a run, causing it to turn sharply from its original path and bound in ever-increasing leaps to the safety of the underbrush.

My ranger had stopped for a moment about halfway down the trail, and turned off to one side. I could see why; just to the left of the trail, the trees thinned enough to see the leading edge of the chasm, starting its slope towards the river. It gratified me, as I looked, to know that even though my ranger was out on patrol, a routine "range" as it were, he (or just as likely she, the boot wasn't too huge) still marveled at the spectacle the job surrounded, and appreciated it for the beauty it was.

Or maybe a bootlace had come undone. I couldn't really say.

All of a sudden the silence I had been enjoying was broken by the roar of the river thousands of feet below. I had come upon the Canyon's edge, and the direct sight-line to the Gunnison allowed a sound like unbroken thunder to reach me. I stepped to the brink, leaned out over a hopefully well-built railing, and looked down.

The sight was truly awesome. Even as well-adapted to vertigo as I was, my heart leapt into my throat as I gazed down to the churning blue-green rapids at the cliff's base. The scene's focus was nearly half a mile down, and still I couldn't help looking at the boiling waters with a sense of unease; even the scramble to the river I had taken that summer had left me unprepared for the sheer inaccessibility of this upper portion of the gorge. The ground left the rim and became nearly vertical until hitting the bottom, with a tiny border of talus near the foaming Gunnison. Here the river was forced into one of its most narrow paths, and surged angrily through the undersized crack. The whole grim and humbling scene repeated itself, in reverse, as my eyes went up the other wall. This was truly a forbidding obstacle, and I began to understand the sense of dread that pervaded the early expeditions and, to an extent, that of Torrence and Fellows.

It was a canyon like no other. Arizona's Grand Canyon is so immense in scale as to forbid the human mind to encompass it; Black Canyon, however, is just barely out of reach. It is small enough to trick you into thinking you can comprehend distances, narrow enough to make you think you could grasp the geologic forces that shaped it. But not quite; looking upstream along the rim, I could just make out the blue roof of the new visitor center, a tenth of the size I would have expected.

I stood at the edge, and let the light breeze and the sound of angry water wrap around me. I tried to take in the magnitude of the scene, thinking of the billions of years it had taken to create and carve these sheer rocks. I thought of the wise Utes who had stayed away from the Canyon, and the white men who couldn't leave it unexplored; my thoughts went to Roubidoux, Gunnison, Hayden, Bryant, Torrence, and Fellows. Each of these men had, with their companions, experienced the Black Canyon as it never would be again: without roads to the rim, or dams to hold back the wild river. They had seen a national treasure before it was recognized and, in the case of Torrence and Fellows, had seen its every face and mood, up close and personal.

I knew then, even as I looked fearfully at the turbulence below, that before I could begin to understand Fellows' actions or motives, I had to see the Canyon as he had. And while plans began to form in my head for the following spring, there was one thought I could not banish from my skull; *"What in hell am I thinking?"*

☾

INTERLUDE 2.

Who, exactly, was William W. Torrence?

This is not as easy a question as it might seem. Unlike Fellows, who seemed to take his role as an object of future historians seriously, Torrence doesn't appear to have kept any papers. There is no collection of Torrence letters in the National Archives; none of his descendants appear to have taken the time to publish a genealogical record.[5] Yet in downtown Montrose, there is a large plaque commemorating the workers of the Uncompahgre Valley Project which names him, as do many texts, the "Father of the Gunnison Tunnel."

Why?

Tracking down Torrence is somewhat problematic. The first record of him anywhere is in Montrose, where in 1897 he became the Superintendent of the Montrose Power and Light Company, or the Montrose P&L. We only know this because of a newspaper article in October, 1905, in the *Press* that mentions his departure after seven years.

Records for Montrose P&L seem to have dropped from the face of the earth, mostly due to the high volume of buyouts to which early Western Colorado power companies were subject. It got its start in early 1889, with a charter grant from the City of Montrose and a capitalization of $10,000, a rather sizable sum at the time. Six local businessmen ran the company: P.A. Hiebler, his brother Alonzo, J.E. McClure, Fred Hamilin, William A. Eckerly, and Charles E. McConnell. The Hiebler brothers owned a planing mill, and it was there that

---

[5] With one exception. A single genealogy buff was kind enough to send me an email that provided me with one incontrovertible fact, something they don't know at the Visitor Center, in Montrose, or anywhere else where they talk about the Black Canyon and the Gunnison Tunnel. the second "W" in William W. Torrence? It stands for "Wellington."

they installed a direct current generator. That generator was run by a water wheel, and by day powered the mill. By night it was used to light up a few dim bulbs in town. There was also a steam engine that could supplement the system during low water, when the wheel wouldn't turn.

In 1892 the whole operation was moved to the local flour mill, where an early irrigation canal brought water from the Uncompahgre River for the wheel. This system was a little more convenient to town, but using the irrigation canal had its own problems, since the farmers took most of the water from it for their fields.

One year later, J.E. McClure's bank failed, and the $10,000 loan was in jeopardy. The man who held the paper was from Denver, one E.S. Kassler, who moved his family out to Montrose to run the power company himself. He did so almost entirely with sheer will until the winter of 1897, when he came into some more money and began improving the system. By 1898 he had poured nearly $15,000 into improvements and new staff, at least one of whom had to be young Torrence.

There is a picture of Torrence I have come across on multiple occasions, showing him leaning against a building in coveralls, holding a pipe wrench in one hand and an enormous pipe-cutter in the other. This was what being "superintendent" was at the time. He was in charge of keeping a water wheel spinning, and of keeping in one piece an underpowered engine running an outdated generator. In July of 1899 there was a city-wide celebration for the installation of the new boiler, a 125 h.p. Corliss, capable of running nearly 300 bulbs. This was the state of affairs with which Torrence dealt on a daily basis.

It seems that he spent his idle moments wandering into the nearby wilderness, becoming something of a mountain man, and someone viewed as extremely capable when faced with difficulty. This undoubtedly was the reason he was selected to join the Pelton party in 1900. He was remembered as personable and temperate by the few who wrote his praises, and the story goes that the Pelton adventurers would surely have perished were it not for Torrence's skill in the outdoors.

That trip had its beginnings in 1896, when prominent local judge John C Bell heard the ravings of miner-cum-farmer F.C. Lauzon during a town meeting. Bell had entered law school lacking a middle initial, and had added the "C" to sound more distinguished; one account by a descendant claimed it stood for "Candy," after his habit of carrying sweets in his pocket at all times. He never wrote the period after the "C." After ten years in Congress he found himself often attending Montrose town meetings. When Lauzon spoke of diverting Gunnison waters into the valley for irrigation, Bell immediately named a number of those present to "fact-finding committees" to look into the matter. One of those named was A.W. Hovey, a farmer whose more adventurous brother M.F. began to organize an expedition into the Canyon slated for 1900.

Hovey's planning attracted the attention of J. E. Pelton, another ex-miner who, after making his fortune in Colorado gold, settled two and a half miles west of Montrose to devote his attentions to growing fruit and raising cattle. Pelton was one of those interesting self-made men who had a penchant for the unusual. In addition to his orchards and cattle, he was the owner of a sizable lake, whose most remarkable feature was that it was entirely artificial. He had it dug and surrounded with trees, and stocked it each year with Eastern brook trout which invariably died in the first good freeze. He also kept a pair of boats in the lake, to row around with your best girl under a parasol in the stern.

Pelton's best girl (and wife) happened to be Swedish-born Katie Anderson, whose brother Eric was another nearby rancher who found himself on the 1900 expedition. Rounding out this foursome was Delta county surveyor John A. Curtis, who had cut his teeth surveying in Wyoming in the 1880s.

Pelton, Hovey, Anderson, and Curtis were well-off, civic-minded men, intent on exploring a canyon that an 1881 Denver and Rio Grande Railroad surveying party had pronounced unfit for humanity. They had each, in their day, had some kind of harrowing adventure in the great unknown; but there was no denying that having along a local, likable, and capable youth like Torrence was extremely attractive. So he joined the party, making them five.

Pelton's lake boats were rechristened the *City of Montrose* and the *John C Bell*, odd names for boats, but good at focusing attention on the driving forces in their campaign. By the time both boats were wrecked in the more narrow stretches of the canyon, and the swirling waters of the Narrows faced them, they were ready for anyone to deliver them home. Local legend evolved to tell the likely story that Torrence found a narrow side canyon that was scalable, and after a doubtless difficult climb and subsequent long hike back to Montrose, everyone had developed an even higher opinion of their young friend.

But Torrence had developed a taste for adventure, and also perhaps for the notoriety his rescue had afforded him. When Fellows advertised in the *Press* for an assistant in his 1901 endeavor, Torrence leapt at the chance. Most of the specifics of this second expedition (e.g. rubber rafts, long ropes, and supply lines) were undoubtedly Torrence's suggestions. The ultimate success of the trip served to further his local image, and probably had a lot to do with it being his face on the plaque in town instead of Fellows'.

By 1905, it seems likely that some degree of his notoriety as an adventurer had died down, and he had focused upon his work in the ever-growing Power and Light Company. His skills had attracted the attention of General Electric in New York, and in October he left Montrose for the Nela Park Lamp Development Laboratory. There he played a part in the development of the mass-produced light bulb.

But the trail, as far as I could see, ended there. Or rather, with a tombstone in Fairmount Cemetery in Denver, "W.W. Torrence, 1872-1921 / Frances Torrence 1872-1948." An obituary in the *Denver Times* in December, 1921:

> . . . With A. Lincoln Fellows, who survives him today and has long been a widely esteemed citizen of Denver, Torrence, then but a young and ambitious engineer, plunged into the dark cañon which seemed twice to invite him to a miserable death by exposure and drowning, and risked his life to explore the forbidding chasm cut deep into the face of nature.
>
> Not once, but many times, this intrepid youth dared and outfought death. Had they lost the gallant fight in 1901

they would have disappeared from the face of the earth until the waters yielded up their dead. As it was, they emerged from the yawning abyss battered and bruised . . . and lived to see a desert converted into a garden as a result of their fearlessness.

. . . Torrence, dead, and Fellows, living, typify the dauntless spirit of the engineer. As a profession, it breeds he-men, men who pioneer and explore, who enter the wilderness and penetrate the fastnesses of the mountains, blazing the way for the comforts and convenience of civilization and opening up new worlds for development.

I imagine Torrence would have appreciated the sentiment.

14.

I required one assistant and in selecting him I made these conditions: First, he must be a good swimmer; strong and athletic; second, he must be unmarried and have no one entirely dependent upon him; third, he must be strictly temperate and a good companion and at all times ready to obey orders; fourth, he must offer his own services unsolicited by me. There were many applications, but from all of them I selected a man whom I had all along hoped would offer his services, William W. Torrence of Montrose, about thirty years of age, who had been a member of the Pelton party during the expedition of the preceding year and fully understood the difficulties and dangers that had to be surmounted.

—A. Lincoln Fellows, 1901

IT WAS 1991, and I was standing in two feet of icy slush and freezing water, peering around a boulder to see my friend downstream.

Michael had his backpack looped over a single shoulder, fearing the worst. In one hand, held high above his head, he had his camera. In the other he wielded a long branch, and was using it to test the depths of the brown, sediment-laden river.

We had come to the canyon of the Paria River, a long, narrow crack that met up with the Colorado River at a place called Lee's Ferry, hoping to find a wonderland where we could train students for Search and Rescue. Michael and I had seen pictures of this place, a canyon whose walls rose hundreds of feet, but where you could stand with a hand on either face. In the center ran the opaque Paria, an immensely silty river, heading downstream and forming the path we would follow. Walking the canyon, we had been told that most of our time would be spent splashing gaily along in the shallow water.

What we didn't know was that we were taking the hike too early in the season. The water that guided us was partially frozen, like a mud smoothie, and the narrow canyon offered only a few hours of sunlight every day. As a result, we had to stop every hundred feet or so, strip off our frozen boots and socks, and make every effort to regain feeling in our toes.

To make matters worse, in the lower reaches of the canyon an occasional boulder had fallen, diverting and often deepening the river. Thanks to the silt, we had no idea how deep the water was. Hence, the stick Michael had in his hand.

Michael had found quicksand off to the right of the boulder, and had backtracked quickly. He was convinced the left route might be passable.

"This looks good," he yelled back. And took a step.

With a yelp, his body disappeared under the freezing water. For a few moments, all that remained in sight was his camera, at the end of his outstretched arm. Then, with a gasp of air and a look of disbelief, he climbed back out into shallower water, soaking wet and cold, running for the nearest tiny patch of sunlight. He shucked his pack and stripped down to warm up on the rock.

The rest of the trip followed a similar pattern, and days later we finally emerged at Lee's Ferry, exhausted and humbled. Michael was a good enough friend to speak to me afterwards, but I had been forced to promise that future trips would be better researched.

Thus, as I plotted Michael's involvement in a trek down Black Canyon, I realized that a serious show of confidence would be essential. The Black Canyon was much bigger, the river much stronger, and the danger much greater should anything go wrong. So I set out to devise a plan of attack.

I recognized Michael as an ideal partner. Not only was he game enough to follow me into the unknown, he was a fabulous photographer in the face of adversity. Michael came from, or at least subscribed to, that school of photography which demanded sacrifice to "get the shot"; I imagined he would probably instinctively protect his camera from a bullet with his own body, like a wartime photojournalist. And even though the Paria trip had ranged from extremely uncomfortable to outright threatening, he had managed to fire off multiple rolls of film, and his slides were breathtaking enough to nearly eclipse the hardships we had experienced.

But I had to ensure that this trip would be planned to minimize our discomfort, and ensure our personal safety to the greatest extent possible. So, I called upon history for some help. I wanted to see how well my selection of Michael as a partner fit with Fellows' expectations of Torrence.

Fellows wanted someone who was a good swimmer, and for obvious reasons, I agreed with him. Michael had already proven himself in that regard.

Fellows also required that his companion be unmarried, and have no one entirely dependent upon him. Marriage had never, to my knowledge, been a high priority in Michael's life, and as a grad student, the karmic balances of provider and supported were already tipped far into his favor. He depended on many, but no one's financial future hinged on his actions.

With respect to Fellows' next requirements, I gave Michael a favorable two out of three; "strictly temperate," yes; "a good companion," by all means; "at all times ready to obey orders," hardly. But in Michael's case, I knew that his suggestions for courses of action were every bit as valid as mine; there was no necessity of obedience.

The last of Fellows' requirements presented a bit of an ethical dilemma. Fellows wanted someone to offer to join his team unsolicited. I, on the other hand, badgered Michael endlessly to accompany me down the canyon. As I considered the requirement, I began to understand it, especially when taken in context with the bit about being unmarried.

Fellows wanted to keep his conscience clear. There was some serious danger involved in getting down Black Canyon in 1901; the river was wild and unpredictable, the terrain rough and ever-changing. The unknown and unknowable factors of the time no doubt put some fear in Fellows that he might not survive the trip; I imagine the last thing he wanted was to feel personally responsible for leading another man to his doom.

Today, there are so many more things known about the Canyon. I had in my possession a detailed topographic map, showing every side canyon, every tiny waterfall, every avenue of escape. A well-placed phone call could tell me, perhaps to the gallon, exactly how fully the river would swell each hour of my trip. I had no need of resupply, being able to carry enough moderately scrumptious freeze-dried food to last a month if necessary. I had the fruits of nearly a century of fabric design, clothing that would keep me warm in practically every climate and condition. And perhaps most importantly, I knew the trip could be done.

But there were still risks. The opportunity to twist or break a limb clambering over cliffsides, the chance to crack a rib against a boulder while swimming the river, the likelihood of suffering some mishap or other that could ruin one's day with frightening speed: all these were in my mind as I wondered how I felt about subjecting Michael to the Black Canyon.

Erin listened patiently as I worried over Michael, having known this man as a dear friend as long as I had. She reminded me that I would follow him to the ends of the earth with the same kind of enthusiasm, support, and trust that he had been exhibiting towards me. I had no need to clear my conscience, she said, because the nature of Michael's and my relationship took care of such silly things as guilt and blame, eradicating them in the larger framework of a good friendship. Or words to that effect.

"Neat," I said. And I called him.

INTERLUDE 3.

In 1894, two men laid a survey line across what would, they surmised, be the location of the future Gunnison Tunnel. Walter Fleming, future captain of the Montrose Fire Department (1896), and Richard Winnerah, future county surveyor (1897), spent the better part of a month sighting on one another through levels and theolodites. In less than a decade, their line was abandoned in favor of one chosen by a federal team from the Reclamation Service.

Ever since, members of the Montrose community had been trying to get back into the act. With the Reverend Mark T. Warner, they managed it quite nicely.

History will forever remember "the Warner Expedition" of 1934. Actually, if history was fair, it would have been called the "Davis Expedition," since the trip was instigated, planned, and largely funded through the efforts of one Robert O. Davis of the U.S.G.S. In fact, the purpose of the trip was to create a topographic map of the newly (since 1933) designated National Monument. To the Reverend's credit, he was a principal mover and shaker in the initial attempts to make the canyon more accessible to the public; through his involvement in the local Lions Club, he was perhaps the one individual most responsible for a dirt road being built to the rim in 1930.

Mark T. Warner was the pastor of the Montrose Presbyterian Church, and by every definition a civic leader. He also, through his time spent in parts of the inner-canyon, managed to get himself included in the six-man party sent down the Gunnison River in July for the purpose of making a map, a task for which he clearly had few skills. His experience as an outdoorsman was well known; however, he was by any reckoning the oldest person on the expedition. My personal conviction was that Warner was brought along for one reason: he was a ton of fun.

Warner was born in Ohio in 1889, which made him forty-five years old by the time of the expedition, and he had never preached anywhere besides Montrose. Throughout the Black Canyon trip, he kept a witty, lively journal, parts of which ended up in the *Montrose Daily Press*, the *Colorado Magazine*, and a book which, although out of print, is still available in reasonable supply from the gift shop in the Visitor Center.

Also on the trip was a forty-four year-old photographer named Dexter B. Walker. His selection was a move of unparalleled brilliance, whether it was realized at the time or not. Walker had a photographic studio in town, and his photos are some of the best I have ever seen. Period. His capacity for composition and lighting put him so ahead of his time in the field of outdoor photography as to make one doubt the date on the bottom of the prints.

Obviously Davis went along. He was in charge, after all. He brought along a pair of rodmen to take care of the actual survey work, Robert Eykyn and Palmer Bowen.

The expedition arranged to have a couple of local boys, Charles and Harry Kane, bring extra food and equipment down from the rim at regular intervals.

And the last member was a young man named Glen Fleming. Of the same Fleming blood as the 1896 Fire Chief? I couldn't find out for sure, but I'd put my money there. Young Fleming was on a summer break from theological seminary, and appears in most of the photos at Rev. Warner's side.

So the Warner Expedition was created, and they set out to pack. From the Reverend's book, it appears the greatest comfort they left at home was the razor, since at one point the Kane brothers were kind enough to bring down that morning's newspaper, as well as a freshly baked cake, courtesy of Mrs. Davis. Despite this apparent luxury, these men did gain a place in history as the first widely-recorded American backpackers to carry salami, the Italian meat product which seems to lack entirely the capacity to spoil.

There were no mishaps to speak of on the trip. A couple of them had stomach problems on the second day, a few had blisters, and most developed sunburn from the 'lunchtime swims' which had been deemed a practical necessity by the group. These dips, the remarkable quantities of food consumed, and the assistance of the Kane brothers with the heavier items: none of it seems to have dimmed the impression of these men as adventurers. In five days, with some members of the group surveying, they made it from what is now East Portal to Red Rock Canyon. A topo map was eventually drawn, and Warner's place in history was secured: his name marks the highest point on the South Rim, as tribute to the work he did in his later years promoting conservation in the Black Canyon. Who has ever heard of Davis?

15.

I NEVER GOT THE HANG of Denver International Airport. It's not that complicated, but as I stood around the baggage claim area waiting for Michael to arrive, I still wondered if I was really in the right place. My wife and I made the drive to Denver to pick up Michael, who somehow had managed to find a week to spend with me. Supposedly he had to work a few days in town finishing some paper or other, but then he would be able to head for the canyon.

I walked down the length of the terminal, squinting at arrival and departure times, scanning the crowd. Usually I spot people after they've already seen me, so I was looking for someone with their arms in the air, even calling my name. Then something made me stop; I turned and looked back.

There was Michael, standing next to his enormous and fully stuffed pack, grinning at me from practically the other end of the terminal. I grinned back, and headed his way.

The next thirty-six hours or so found my partner slaving over a computer; his paper was a little more incomplete than he had let on. But nine pots of coffee later he prevailed and, snuggling a pillow in the back seat, managed to sleep most of the six hour drive back to the Western Slope.

That evening, we spread out our gear in the garage and opened cans of beer. Most of what we had to bring was pretty basic stuff: sleeping bags, lightweight air mattresses, a tiny tent, cookstove, pots, pans, spare clothes and, in Michael's case, a smorgasbord of cameras, lenses, and film. But two things in particular made packing interesting; the inclusion of a hundred-foot rope "for emergencies," and waterproofing everything.

This last was a tricky proposition, since we only had two rubber drybags. Those bags were immediately relegated to protecting the camera equipment. That left plastic zipper sacks and garbage bags for everything else. We stuffed our sleeping bags into their stuffsacks with the garbage bags inside, the idea being that the plastic would be better protected. We put things like clothes and food into zipper sacks, along with items like notebooks and maps, and I coiled the rope inside a plastic-lined stuffsack.

Along with waterproofing came the subject of flotation. We knew we would be spending a lot of time swimming in very cold water, so a little edge would be important. To this end we each brought lifejackets for ourselves, and strapped "wacky noodles" to the packs. "Wacky noodles" are extruded foam pool toys, about a yard long and four inches or so wide. They look like brightly colored foam pipe insulation, and run about ten dollars apiece. I sliced my noodles in half and stuffed them into each other, to make it easier to attach them to my pack's frame. Michael was able to fold his over and slip them inside loops on either side of his internal frame pack. We were convinced that the flotation provided by the air trapped inside the packs, combined with the added boost from the noodles, would be enough to keep the things more or less above water.

Sipping beer in the warm garage, it didn't seem too important to get an early start. Michael was still dragging a little from his marathon writing session, and our schedule allowed for five or six solid days in the canyon. Fellows and Torrence spent ten days going from Cimarron to Red Rock Canyon, but we wouldn't be going as far. Starting at Cimarron, these days would present something of a challenge, since the better part of the route Fellows and Torrence followed sits under thousands of gallons of reservoir water.

We would begin at the same place the Warner expedition started, and where Fellows and Torrence spent two nights and a day resting. East Portal sits at the junction of the Gunnison River and a steep side canyon, where a treacherous road leads from the rim. The altitude at East Portal is 6,474 feet above sea level, 1,850 feet below the rim. Our ultimate destination was Chukar, a boating put-in with a fairly decent access road. Chukar lies below Red Rock and just outside the park boundary, a little over eleven walking miles and a thousand vertical feet downstream from East Portal. Warner and his group made this kind of distance in five days, and Fellows and Torrence hiked from "Boat Landing" (as it was then known) to Red Rock in four. It didn't seem too optimistic to think we could make it in six days, especially since we weren't carrying survey equipment.

Erin brought out microwaved burritos for us, and we all munched happily; the weather forecast was ideal, the Gunnison River was running acceptably low, and, most importantly, a year of waiting had at last come to an end.

Finally, we were going to tackle the Black Canyon.

16,

Exploration was actually commenced August 12, 1901. At the head of the Grand Canon of the Gunnison is the mouth of the Cimarron River. The Denver and Rio Grande Railroad comes out of the Black Canon of the Gunnison to this point, then climbing out of the canon by way of the Cimarron and one of its tributaries. It was at this point that our toilsome journey was commenced. The conductor kindly stopped the train upon the exact spot where I told him we wished to get off. Turning immediately down the canon, we started upon our perilous journey.

—A. Lincoln Fellows, 1901

FRIDAY, SEPTEMBER 4TH, 1998. Michael reminded me it was author Richard Wright's birthday. We woke up late, wolfed down a quick breakfast, did a final check on our packs, and headed out. Erin drove us to the visitor center, where we waited to pick up our backcountry permit. I had been in e-mail contact with Paul, but unfortunately he was working elsewhere that day; ultimately, a ranger I had never met signed our permit, and cautioned us to "be careful."

To get to East Portal from the visitor center, we had to backtrack almost to the park entrance, then veer off onto a smaller road that disappeared over the horizon. As we drove over the edge, we could see the pavement vanish and reappear behind multiple switchbacks, winding its dizzying way into the gorge. My wife shifted down to second gear, then first, riding the brake nearly all the way down as the incline crept above fifteen percent. As we approached hairpin turns, she would slow to glance at convex mirrors placed next to the road, to check for traffic coming the other way.

We reached the bottom around noon, and for the first time could see the river up close. We drove to the tiny campground and parked at the very end, as far downriver as vehicles could go; I stepped out of the truck and onto the dusty road, slamming the door and listening to the sound echo off the far canyon wall. The quiet was broken slightly by the low ruffle of the placid Gunnison, and by the occasional chirp of some hidden bird which sounded uncannily like a basketball shoe coming to a sudden stop on a waxed floor.

But it was the river that caught and held our attention. At East Portal it was deep, green, and slow-moving, eerily calm. The size of it, the sheer volume of water represented an enormous potential force, a violence contained and plodding along. You could almost feel it beneath your feet, as if the river was pushing against the banks, rumbling discontentedly, waiting. Michael and I stared for a moment, then broke the spell and unloaded our packs.

Erin took our picture and, with an extended arm, Michael snapped off a shot of all three of us, two explorers and our one-woman support team. Michael's family are all travelers, and he explained that when someone left for a long trip, his mother would say a little blessing over them. Following suit, Erin poured water from our bottles into a film canister, and threw it over us, saying, "Go like water, come like water." We all smiled; it felt good, right. One final round of hugs, and we headed downriver along the south bank, waving back at my wife and civilization.

It felt surprisingly good to be carrying weight on my shoulders. I could tell by Michael's demeanor that he was enjoying it, too; we talked back and forth as we walked, immersed in the simple pleasure of a journey. Along the bank we followed a faint trail, most likely used by fishermen. The path would climb up ten feet or so to go over some rocky bank, then crash through thin bushes to return to the water's edge. To our right, the river began to churn a little more insistently, but we hardly noticed. The going was easy, the sun was shining; it was a perfect day for a hike.

Just a few hundred yards in, we came upon our first obstacle. The trail ended abruptly where our little bench ran straight into a cliff. There was no way to climb around the cliff, so we looked downriver. Our two options were to float alongside the cliff on the south side until it ended, which seemed pretty far down, or to swim across to the north side. The second choice seemed better, since the going looked pretty straightforward on the other side, and plus the river seemed to get rougher just a little way down. Also, since the weather was unconscionably pleasant, it seemed as good a time as ever for our first swim.

We shucked the packs and strapped on our lifevests; I found myself fiddling with my "noodles" and setting my pack into the water slowly, in the hope of keeping my things as dry as possible. Miraculously, the contraption actually floated, as did Michael's; we pushed them into the river gently and waded after them, whooping a little about the cold.

Michael thought I should go first, so I waded out as far as I could comfortably touch bottom, then pushed off and started kicking behind my pack. The cold punched the breath out of my lungs, and I remember thinking we would have to go back for wetsuits. But slowly my body started to adjust, and as I kicked towards the south shore I began to feel more confident and looked back towards Michael. He had started across, observing my apparent success, and was kicking hard and even pulling a sort of half-crawl through the water with one arm.

All at once I felt the river bed through the toes of my boots, and stood up, hauling my soaked backpack onto the shore and collapsing next to it. I began warming up almost immediately on the sun-cooked rocks as Michael pulled himself and his gear up next to me. We were both grinning like crazy men, elated that the first hurdle had been so easily overcome. Now we knew we could swim the river with our packs, and that everything floated and appeared no worse for the experience. At that moment, it seemed like anything was possible.

> The packs on our shoulders were not light, although we had limited their size as much as we could. It was frequently necessary to wade through deep water, even where we were obliged to swim, and all walking was along boulders which formed the talus of the canon walls. Easy walking was never to be found unless it was a very few feet upon some gravel bar. We would proceed along one side of the river until we came to a point where it was absolutely necessary either to cross, or to swim for some distance out into the stream, making as rapid progress as we could.
>
> —A. Lincoln Fellows, 1901

I remember the rest of the day as a constant scramble, punctuated by an occasional swim. The boulders nearest the river were worn smooth around the edges, making them exceptionally slippery when our feet were wet. This turned out to be most of the time; it seemed as if every time our clothes threatened to dry off, some irregularity in our steps would shift the weight of the backpacks and release a small torrent of water from an unseen reservoir inside. Once Michael bent to tie his bootlace, and at least a gallon of river water poured onto his head from the hollow center of his "noodles"; apparently they had filled during a previous swim, and he had been carrying the extra weight for some time. A few strategically knifed holes in the foam created a better flow-through, and took care of that problem at least.

We passed a fly-fisherman on the north side, and floated downstream past his wicker basket to a good-sized sand beach, where we stopped for a snack. It was around 3:00, and the sun was still falling directly on the bottom of the canyon, so after a quick bite we pulled out the cameras and took pictures for a few minutes. I waded out into the river to take a water-level snap up the canyon; Michael set up various shots of the cliffs around us, which had become increasingly impressive as we made our way down.

No matter what the canyon floor looked like, rocks, gravel, or sand, at some point on the way up to the rim it would turn into a vertical cliff face, looming above as if placed specifically to remind us how cut off we were from the rest of the world. Sometimes the cliffs would curve off into little mounds, like haystacks, and often the end would come in a sharp pinnacle. Church spires, needles, javelins; every description I had read rang true, and every time I looked up I was astounded by the jagged skyline, the torn strip of blue sky the canyon allowed us. Birds darted here and there, and now and again the silhouette of an eagle or a falcon passed far, far overhead. But for the most part we were alone, and the sound of the increasingly turbulent river began to cut us off even from each other, as we had to yell to be heard above the water's roar.

The day wore on, and as we clambered over a particularly large boulder field, we began to worry that we wouldn't come across a good place to camp for the night. But then, just as it began to darken, we pulled ourselves up onto an enormous flat rock practically wedged between the canyon walls. We looked at one another, grinned, and decided to make our first camp there.

The top of the rock was about 30 by 40 feet, with a flat spot on one end that fit the footprint of our tent perfectly. The platform sat fifty feet above the river, straight up; six inches from the corner of our tent was a drop-off into the wildest rapid we had seen yet. The water below was forced into a small space between rocks, resulting in a tiny but extremely violent water chute that terminated in a recirculating wave river-runners call a hole, or a "keeper," since anything that floats into it—logs, boats, people—tends to stay churning around for quite a while.

The other side of the platform gently sloped towards the river (and our tent), so we designated it a cooking space and stripped off our wet clothes. Michael and I began pulling sacks from our backpacks, inspecting which things had stayed dry; on this first day we batted about .500, with about half of our things getting pretty much soaked through. Michael's synthetic sleeping bag, for example, had become an enormous sponge, and had to be spread out on the rock, but thankfully my own down bag was bone dry. We set up the stove and cookset, and took turns cooking and hanging wet clothes on every available surface. In ten minutes we had transformed our rock into what looked like one giant laundry line, and we laughed at how pitiful the whole setup was against the backdrop of such beautiful scenery.

I had nearly finished cooking the pasta when Michael asked where his sleeping bag had gone. Assuming I had put it in the tent after it dried, he hadn't asked earlier when he couldn't find it; but when I expressed total ignorance, we began scouring the rock. The constant noise from the river meant we could barely hear each other's yells, much less something so subtle as an evening wind blowing across camp. After a few frantic moments, we spotted the bag on a little ledge below our rock, not too hard to get to, and still dry. After that we started tying things up, or weighing them down with stones to prevent another jailbreak.

Dinner went down famously, like meals on the trail do, and we settled onto our backs to watch the moon rise. I produced a small flask, and the conversation drifted through family, old friends, wives and girlfriends, and ultimately came to rest on the incredible beauty of the scene around us. We were just two days before a full moon, and as it came up we watched the silver light creep down the canyon walls until it struck us, bright as anything. Inspired, I pulled out my journal to write by moonlight, and Michael moved off a few paces and began playing a little flute he had brought along.

The scene was fantastic; everything was bathed in magic. I could just make out the faint strains of "Go Tell Aunt

Rhody" over the white roar of the Gunnison. It was so subtle that I could almost still hear the music, even after Michael had stopped playing. When we finally crawled into our sleeping bags, we were tired, but warm and happy. It was one of the nicest evenings I could remember, and I fell into a contented sleep, looking forward to the morning with the purest optimism.

17.

Our surroundings were of the wildest possible description. The roar of the water falls was constantly in our ears and the walls of the canon towering half mile in height above us, were seemingly vertical. Occasionally a rock would fall from one side or the other, with a roar and crash, exploding like a ton of dynamite when it struck bottom, making us think our last day had come. At times the canon would become so narrow that it would almost, but never quite, be possible to step across the river. At times, great gorges of rock that had fallen in from the sides would hem in the water to such an extent that it would be nearly concealed. On the second day of our trip we were so unfortunate as to get into a veritable cul-de-sac from which it took us the entire afternoon to extricate ourselves, camping that night just across the river from where we had eaten our lunch at noon. Our most dangerous work, possibly, was that of clambering along the sides of precipices, traversing old mountain sheep trails, at points where it was impracticable to swim without too great danger to life and limb.

—A. Lincoln Fellows, 1901

SATURDAY, SEPTEMBER 5TH. We woke up late to a bright morning, everything well illuminated long before the sun actually peeked over the rim. I started some water for coffee while Michael began taking down the tent. Over our granola breakfast, we came to the conclusion that we had made good time yesterday, and didn't need to get too early a start. A few pictures seemed to be in order, so we thoroughly documented the setup of our dramatic first campsite.

We were nearly packed up when a head wearing a bright pink helmet peeked over our rock. As we stared in disbelief, a kayaker appeared, carrying his boat over one shoulder. He was followed by another, and another; in all there were eight boaters portaging around our rapid, heading downstream.

We talked briefly, as well as we could over the roar. They knew about our trip, and eyed our enormous packs warily; it was one of those situations where each group thinks the other is completely out of their minds. As the kayakers started setting up cameras on our rock platform, it became apparent that one of them was planning to run the rapid below. I couldn't believe it; the keeper at the end would be nearly impossible to avoid, and hitting it would necessitate a quick rescue, and probably an evacuation.

But no one else thought it was strange, and the man sealed his spray-skirt around his boat and shoved off, paddling madly to reach the opposite shore. He disappeared behind a rock, showing up about a minute later out of his boat, scouting the run from the other side.

After a few moments of inspection he seemed satisfied, and disappeared again to wherever he had landed his boat. Michael adjusted his camera and stood near the kayakers, sensing a good shot in the works.

Suddenly the sleek red boat burst from behind a boulder, and was in the rapid. The man took strong, long strokes with his paddle, aiming just to the right of the rapid's tongue. He slid his boat down the chute and veered off fiercely, with one last pull neatly avoiding the keeper and parking himself in an eddy at the bottom of the rapid.

It all happened so fast, and so flawlessly. The guy made it look easy. All the kayakers smiled, bid farewell, and hiked their boats downstream to where their heroic comrade waited patiently. They slid into the water and paddled off, around the corner and out of sight in minutes. Michael noted that they were making much better time than we were, so we decided to get a move on.

Hefting my pack, it seemed that my load was a little lighter that morning. We agreed it was probably because it had time to dry, and would most likely gain back twenty or thirty pounds after the day's first swim (sadly, that prediction turned out true). We took one last look around our cheery little spot, and turned downstream.

It was another morning of negotiating the smooth boulders near the river, climbing up one and sliding down another. I started noticing little scrapes down the rocks, and finally figured out what they were. Some previous expedition had taken nearly the same route as we were, picking the same boulders to climb or go around; it was likely a trip taken in winter, because the scrapes I saw were from hobnailed boots. I imagined the scratches were made in the winter of 1881 by the Bryant party, but of course I had no way to prove it; just because no one I knew wore hobnails didn't mean that no one did. It was still nice to think about.

Around noon we reached our first swim, a quick little float below a boulder field we thought would take too long to climb. This illustrated one of the differences between myself and Michael. I hated climbing over the talus slopes, where the boulders rested on top of one another so precariously. You step on one, and it's solid; step on another, and it moves. Sometimes it would move its neighbors, and if the chain of events extended far enough, you had something of a rockslide on your hands. When I considered that some of the rocks were as big as mobile homes, I decided that swimming was vastly preferable.

But Michael didn't see it that way; he was much more comfortable with the climbing aspects of the hike than I was. Michael's experiences over the past few years included a lot of technical climbs, playing around on glaciers and the like. He could get going quickly when he sensed movement underfoot, and never gave it a second thought. He would start traversing a small cliff with an inch of ledge to it, and get halfway across before realizing that a minor wade was both easier and safer. To his credit, he usually deferred judgment to me, which gave me no end of relief.

So we pushed off into the river, and floated quickly past our obstacle. I stood up on a gravel bar and reached out to grab Michael, who had floated a little farther and was on his way toward a little rapid. Soggy and heavy, we continued down.

We came upon a thicket of river grass on the north shore inside a bend in the river, with foliage eight feet tall and impossible to see through. Since the ground underneath was flat, we whacked our way through and, roughly in the middle, we came upon what looked like a campsite. On one end of that, we found what appeared to be a grave.

A carefully piled mound of rocks bore a wooden marker, into which were painstakingly carved the words, "Larry, 1954-1996." I didn't know quite what to make of it, and neither did Michael. The site was littered with empty cans and bottles, a gear bag hanging in a tree, and a sleeping bag stuck under an overhang in what looked like a pretty permanent arrangement; there was evidence of a fire, and to my thinking a pretty recent habitation. Considering this, we elected to move on quickly, not being comfortable with the idea of running into whoever lived there.

We crossed back to the south shore just downstream, and hiked a little further before spotting a family on the north side near a trail that came down from the opposite rim, apparently picnicking on a large rock. We waved, and they watched passively while we shucked our packs, strapped on lifevests and swam around a cliff on our side, getting out, putting our packs back on and continuing on down the canyon. I still wonder what they thought of us.

Around 2:30 we passed a couple having lunch on our side of the river, and it started to dawn upon me that we might not be as far along as we thought. After passing two more groups and running into a developed campsite, it was confirmed: we had only reached the Gunnison route, directly below the visitor center, and farther above the Narrows than I wanted to be so late in the day. My vision had been that we would go through the Narrows and on down to Painted Wall that afternoon, but, as we quickly downed some jerky and dried fruit, it became obvious to us both we'd be lucky to make it anywhere near the Narrows before dark.

The campsite at the base of the Gunnison route was nicely put together, so we took the opportunity to sit on comfortable benches and readjust our packs. By now we had our hike-to-swim transitions moving pretty fast; Michael had even taken to wearing his lifevest while walking, just for the sake of convenience. I had stopped being overly careful when setting my pack in the water, since the smallest wave would crash over the top anyway and ruin any chances of keeping things dry. Satisfied, we buckled up and headed out, leaving behind both questioning daytrippers and the safest, most well-marked route to the South rim.

Just downstream we came upon a cliff that we needed to swim past, so we dropped our packs and got ready. But there was a new problem; the current in the river was such that for the first time, the water next to the wall was moving *upstream*. It was so strong that it pushed me back onto the shore and against the wall, in fact in every direction but where we wanted to go. We stood in the waning afternoon sunlight trying to figure a way through; I leapt into the icy water with a strap over my shoulder and swam as hard as I could, thinking to reach the other side and pull Michael and the packs after me. But as hard as I pulled, I couldn't fight the current. Exhausted, I trudged back onto shore.

Michael took the strap, and waded in. Waist deep, he found handholds and footholds good enough to pull against the force of the water, and after much effort made it rock-climber style to the other side. I lashed the packs together, and held on as he pulled me through. Splashing up to land, we rested for a moment, but moved on quickly; without direct sun, it was taking longer to dry off and warm up. We needed to keep hiking.

We hadn't gone far before we reached another rapid system, hemmed in by cliffs. We dropped the packs and studied it, yelling ideas into each other's ears and walking up and down its length. By the time we figured out a plan, it was too late in the day to try anything; a small patch of flat sand we spotted just upriver looked like the only place anywhere nearby to pitch the tent, so we elected to use it. We hiked back up to that spot and started making camp.

It took a little work, kicking stones around and pulling an occasional branch out of the sand, but finally we made a space large enough for our little tent. I set it up, and Michael went to work, running straps all over camp to hang up wet gear. We found nails and stakes pounded into the cliff next to our tent, and ran lines from them for wet socks, shorts, shirts, and everything else that was unfortunate enough to get a dunking that day.

Once again dinner was delicious, but our conversation that night was a little more muted. We watched a spectacular moonrise, and Michael even managed to set up for a few nighttime pictures; but we were both thinking about the next morning's crossing. It wouldn't be extremely difficult, we hoped, or too technical. But we knew that there would be no way to get back upstream afterwards. That crossing would be a final commitment to the Narrows and whatever lay beyond, and as I scribbled in my journal and listened to Michael's flute, I thought about Ultima Thule, the end of the Greek's explored world. Fellows crossed past his world's Ultima Thule at the Narrows itself; we would be crossing ours tomorrow.

IX,

The canon, heretofore comparatively open with walls having slopes of about 1 to 1 and covered with spruce and pine timber, with here and there groves of aspen and an undergrowth of oak brush, now became more and more rugged. The geological formation was of gneiss and mica schist and the apparently vertical cliffs, instead of being met with occasionally, now became almost continuous. At times we would traverse along reaches looking like mill ponds with the sky and canon walls reflected in the depth of the blue water, but again we would come to rapids and water falls as turbulent as the waters of Lodore.

—A. Lincoln Fellows, 1901

SUNDAY, SEPTEMBER 6TH. For the first time we rose early, ate quickly, and were packed up and headed out before the sun reached our campsite. I had slept well, and felt confident about the morning's crossing. Michael had put on his lucky R.E.M. t-shirt, and I had slipped my air mattress between my pack and frame, making for even more buoyancy. We were loaded for bear, and ready for the day.

There would be, we had previously decided, two parts to this crossing. First, we would have to slide into the main current upstream, and swim like crazy to reach a gravel island in the center of the river. After that, we would walk to the lowest point on the island, and one of us would swim to the north shore carrying a line. From there he would pull across the packs, and the other person if necessary.

As we walked up to our planned point of entry, the waves looked bigger than I remembered. I wondered if the water had risen during the night; it would not have been unheard of for the dam upstream to change its flow after midnight. Either way, it didn't really matter. This was the only way across, so it was the way we would go.

Once again Michael got me to go first, and in I went. The bitter cold first thing in the morning was nearly blinding, and as I kicked towards the island, I noticed I was picking up speed in a strange direction. Any destination besides the island was unacceptable; the rapids on either side were enormous. I kicked faster and harder, starting to panic a little; suddenly I felt my knee drive into a rock, and that dull kind of pain you get when you're really cold sent a shock through my already aggravated system. I stood up in swift, shallow water, almost losing my pack before shouldering it up to the island. More or less secure, I looked back to see how my partner was faring.

Michael had previously been uncomfortable swimming with just one arm, and having to use the other to hold onto his backpack; as a remedy, for this crossing he had looped a strap over his head and shoulder to keep both arms free. I could tell almost right away that this hadn't been a good idea; as he leapt into the river, his pack took a different route downstream than his body. I realized with horror he was being choked by the strap as he tried to swim.

I stood on shore feeling helpless as he struggled with the webbing, finally getting it up over his head. By this time, he had drifted off course considerably, and I was yelling at him to step it up, to get to the left quickly. He started pulling and kicking as fast as he could, but he wasn't making progress quickly enough. I waded out into the current as far as possible, and stretched out my hand in case I had to grab him before he swept past. But at the last second he managed to swim himself to safety, standing up and lunging towards the island on foot.

We were both completely frozen, feeling dangerously numb and awfully banged up. It was all we could do to leave our packs at the low end of the island and stumble into the center, shivering, to wait for sunlight to hit us. The morning wind blew cold against our wet clothes, and we watched as the sun's rays slowly, slowly made their way across the canyon walls down to where we stood, shoulders hunched, inches from the river. After what felt like an eternity, the sun broke over the rim and spilled warmth down upon us, and we stood with our arms outstretched like birds, like holy men deep in worship, eyes closed, feeling every inch of our skin and praising the light, the heat. Eventually we were warm again, and set out to retrieve our packs and negotiate the second part of the crossing.

Between the island and the north shore ran a plume that was at most twenty feet across. The water was very swift, and I took the strap and jumped in upstream, making quickly for the other side. I reached the gravel bar almost immediately, stood up and gave Michael a high sign. He clipped the other end to the two packs, pushed them into the river, and watched as they went down the chute and swung neatly over to my side. Then he jumped in and swam; we were across, and it was almost 10:00.

The next few hours were brutal. Any semblance of an easy route was gone; we were constantly slogging up and down boulders and rockfields, between thorn-covered trees and through frighteningly strong spider webs. At times we would climb hundreds of feet above the river to avoid some spectacular rapid, only to slip and slide back down the other side, take a quick swim, and do it all again. Some of these rapids were unbelievable; the systems centered around falls of four feet or so, churning into huge white-green, foaming pillows of turbocharged water. The sound was entirely deafening at river level, and still dominant as we climbed high above on some talus slope. The boulders through this section seemed even less stable than those earlier, and nearly every step produced some terrifying low scraping noise from deep inside the pile, threatening to send the whole mess, including us, into the Gunnison.

But although it was unnerving, the views were spectacular. The cliffs on either side were sheer, smooth, and steep, running all the way to the rim thousands of feet above. The various falls and rapids were beautifully revealed by the bright mid-morning sunshine, and we stopped in what would, under other circumstances, have seemed ridiculously unsafe places to take photographs, trying to capture as much of it all as possible.

We crested one hill to find our chosen route would now have to head nearly straight down, following a wash from some long-ago flash flood; we were about to start our sliding way to the bottom when we stopped and looked downstream. The canyon seemed to close up, the walls moving nearer and nearer to one another, making it look as if the water simply ended a few hundred yards down. The river was now a source of constant violence, and we could hear mixed in with the noise of water the sound of stones scraping past each other in the current, and the occasional deep thunk as something more substantial shifted underwater.

Clearly there was going to be a difficult swim ahead, so while Michael stayed up high to take a few pictures, I skied down the slope on flat feet, coming to a jarring halt on a pile of sand at the bottom. As I walked into the clearing, for the first time since East Portal I knew exactly where we were.

Below the rapids, the canyon narrowed to what I figured to be exactly forty feet.

19.

When about noon, we reached the lowest point attained by earlier explorers and saw before us the mighty jaws, past which there was to be no escape, I believe I might be pardoned for the feeling of nervousness and dread which came over me for the first time. It was not so much for myself that I feared, but because I was leading another man into a place from which there might be no escape.

—A. Lincoln Fellows, 1901

IT WAS AROUND TWO O'CLOCK.

I took one quick look at the rapids and decided I had to eat something. The roar of water was everywhere, and as I sat down to burrow in my pack for food, Michael came sliding over the rocks above. He dropped his pack and stood next to me, staring downriver.

We had reached the Narrows.

Nervously chewing on jerky, we surveyed the situation. About three hundred feet downstream was the actual Narrows, the point where the canyon slimmed down to a precise forty feet, and the cliffs on either side ran straight to the rim 1,725 feet above. The water between the cliffs seemed almost placid, a deep blue calm that, taken by itself, wouldn't be any problem floating through.

The issue, as we now saw, was not so much the Narrows itself, but the approach. We stood on a tidy sandbar on the north bank, and from the lowermost point we could see right

127

through the chasm to a few giant boulders in the river downstream. Once we were directly upstream of the Narrows on the south side, there would be an easy float for fifty feet or so to a gravel beach along the same side. But our little sand bar paralleled only about half the length of a difficult and complex rapid system, which gave up probably thirty feet of elevation along fifty yards of river. Crossing to the south side for our Narrows float was going to be the hard part.

We anxiously discussed our options. The first plan involved standing at the lowest point on our sandbar with the coiled 100-foot rope. I would loop one end over my shoulder and leap into what appeared to be the deepest water in the rapid, making straight for the other side as quickly as possible. Once there, I would lash off the rope and pull Michael and the packs over. There were, unfortunately, all kinds of problems with this plan; there was no guarantee I could make the swim, no way to tell if we had quite enough rope, and no way of knowing how much rope the current would take as I swam across. Further, even if the rope didn't drag me downstream into one of the uglier and more dangerous rapids, there was no way to know for sure that once across I'd be able to pull Michael and the packs to safety. The worst-case scenarios were unacceptable, so we looked for another solution.

The next idea was just for me to swim across, and have Michael throw the rope. The same uncertainties applied, however, this time with the added possibility of permanently separating myself from Michael and the packs. That would nearly qualify as a disaster.

Finally we settled on trying to cross at the very beginning of the rapids, as far upstream as we could get. On our side, it looked like we could wade fairly far into the current on a sub-merged sandbar, and jump into a little chute of fast water that ran alongside the cliff on the south side. The chute ran right past a small eddy, where it looked as if we could get out of the current and climb onto the shore; however, making that eddy was critical, as just downstream the rapids became unswim-mable. If we missed the shore, we were unquestionably headed for broken ribs or worse. So we decided to make sure we wouldn't miss that eddy.

While Michael strapped the packs together with webbing, I began stacking the rope on top of them, putting one looped end over my shoulder. At the other end, Michael clipped the webbing to the rope. The plan was to wade out as far as we could; I would jump into the current with the rope, make for the eddy downstream, secure myself, and start hauling in rope. Michael would wait until the rope went taut, then shove the packs into the chute's current, following at a safe distance.

It was now four o'clock.

We started across the submerged sandbar, pushing our packs in front of us. The water was extremely cold, and the added tension seemed to drop the temperature further. About fifteen feet from shore, we stood waist deep, just out of reach of the main current. I watched the rapid churn in front of my eyes, getting colder and colder. Suddenly the water surged, and a wave shoved against us, testing our footing. We stood firm, but the packs were jostled and the stacked rope spilled into the current, uncoiling and heading downstream. We grabbed it quickly and began restacking it on the packs, but we were getting colder every second we stood in the water. Finally we were ready again, and before another surge could wreck our setup, I braced for the jump. Michael gave me a nod, and I shoved off into the current.

I bobbed over waves in the chute, watching the cliff face rocket past me. In seemingly no time at all, I reached the eddy, and swam as hard as I could for the south wall. I made it, but the little rock alcove that formed the eddy was smaller than I had thought; there was barely enough room to wedge myself in, still half-underwater and freezing, and start pulling in the rope.

I hauled as fast as I could. The drag on the rope was huge, and I could vaguely see that the current had caught much of the rope and was dragging it back across into the rapids. I clenched my teeth and pulled, the rope falling slack near my feet. For a moment I thought I was going to foul myself on the extra line, and I shook my legs to get the coils untangled from my feet. I looked up and saw the packs float by at high speed, way out of the main chute and heading straight for the rapids.

My adrenalin skyrocketed; I knew what was going to happen next. I reexamined my footing, tried to get a better grip on the rock face. I pulled in rope as fast as I could, looking for a place to lash it off; there was none. Suddenly I was out of rope. The line went taut as the full force of the current slammed into the packs, pulling me briefly to my feet before I sank back into my perch, a death grip on the rope.

The packs were in the center of the rapids, the water splashing and churning around them. The rope had caught on something just upstream, and it seemed that the tension I kept on the rope held them in place. I sat amazed by the whole scene as Michael came sputtering around the corner and into the eddy. He quickly explained he hadn't been able to hold on, that the rope took the packs into the current right after I jumped. I climbed a little higher on the rock to make room for him to get mostly out of the water, and once he was secure handed him the rope.

I yelled into his ear that I would try to get below this set of rapids, that he should wait a few minutes and then let go. The only chance for retrieving the packs was that maybe I could grab the rope in a small calm spot before they reached the Narrows. Michael nodded, and we agreed upon three minutes as our time frame. We each started counting seconds.

The rock above my perch was slick and smooth, and topped with thorny bushes. Soaked and cold as I was, the only way up was through a ten-foot crack in the boulder, and I chimneyed up with my feet flat against the opposing wall. Once up, I crashed through thick branches and slipped on a patch of moss, dropping down to river level on the other side.

I stumbled out to the river's edge. From this vantage I could see the packs upriver, bobbing violently in the current; I couldn't see Michael. Nearly four minutes had passed, and I began to wonder why he hadn't let go of the rope. A wind came up, and I shivered; it was getting late, and nowhere around here looked good for camping. The "gravel beach" I stood on was pocked with car-sized boulders (another trick of perspective), and looking downstream through the Narrows I could see they became even larger and less friendly.

The packs hadn't moved. I was steeling myself to climb back over and see what had happened when Michael appeared from behind the nearest boulder, cold and wide-eyed. I looked back and forth between the packs and my partner, and grimly realized what had happened.

Michael's account confirmed my fears; he had counted out three minutes, and let go of the rope. The current had taken away his end, but the packs didn't budge; somehow, the force of the river on the long end of the rope created enough tension within the system to keep the line from slipping over the rock. We climbed back over the boulders and shimmied down the crack to get a better look, and the situation was clear.

Our gear was as good as gone. Michael's tragically excellent knots were getting tighter by the minute, and there was no way to swim out and free the line. The rapids were too swift, and the likelihood of serious injury was greater here than anywhere else on the river so far. Even if we had managed to get out there and cut the rope, there was an awfully good chance that the packs would have become caught up again a little farther down.

We stared for a full minute, neither of us speaking. We knew what had just happened had ended the trip. We had no food, and no way to purify drinking water. The sun was going down, and we had nothing but shorts, t-shirts, and lifejackets to keep us warm. The only piece of gear either of us had left was our river knives, clipped to our life vests in the event we had to free ourselves from a fouled rope. The Canyon was getting darker, and we had run out of options. We had to try to climb out.

Legends existed of a party which many years before had attempted to pass through the jaws of the canon which now appeared to be closing in upon us. The legend runs that they lost their entire outfit, with one of their party, and being unable to retrace their steps, had, with the uttermost difficulty, scaled the sides of the canon. Pelton's party had reached this point with their second boat; they, too, had abandoned everything and climbed out of the canon, glad to escape with their lives. Their leader had told me that it was impossible for a man to pass through the gorge and live.

—A. Lincoln Fellows, 1901

IT SEEMED AS IF WE STOOD THERE FOR YEARS.

I was as choked up as I can ever remember being. Losing the backpacks meant losing the goal of finishing the canyon, of making it through to the end. The lack of completion, the sense of failure was overwhelming for a moment. Michael and I looked at each other, simultaneously envisioning dramatic plans to rescue the equipment while knowing, wholly and completely, that there was no chance of that now. The sun slipped a little lower, and a wind came up the canyon. The shivering of our bodies pushed us to action, and we headed downstream.

We scrambled over boulders, pushed through brambles, and stomached our way up and down slippery slopes, heading for the next side canyon downriver. All the while, I was racking my brain, trying to see a map in my head. I remembered being in the National Archives, looking at that detail from 1904, or 1905 maybe, that was an exceptionally well drawn map of this exact part of the canyon. It was a Fellows creation, and it had a lot to do with the feasibility study for the dam at the Narrows; it was, in fact, the only map I had found more detailed than the USGS topo maps available in the visitor's center. I remembered seeing on this map a scalable side canyon just a few hundred feet below the Narrows.

The problem was my photocopy of the map was in my backpack.

Michael and I discussed it. My memory of the map told me that the side canyon we could barely see across the river was the way out; the trouble was neither of us could see well past the first few yards of the route, and couldn't tell if it actually led anywhere. The other problem was that crossing to the other side was a risk, both in the danger of the attempt and the realization that getting back to the side we were on was unlikely. But the sun was still going down, and we had to get somewhere. Michael decided to leave the call to me. We headed down to the water's edge to see how to get across.

The river here was extraordinarily loud, and getting right up next to it we had to shout inches from each others' ears again. There really only seemed to be one place where we had a prayer of getting across, just below a flume that dropped ten or fifteen feet. We would have to start at the top of a boulder, run down it, leap as far into the river as possible, and make for the other side as quickly as we could, avoiding another waterfall and rapids about thirty feet below. Just to complicate things, the boulder we would launch ourselves from was covered in moss and slippery as anything; there would be no stopping once we started down the slope. The historical irony of "The Leap" was not lost on me.

The swimming part worried us both, and since the last rapid we had begun to doubt our ability to gauge the speed of a particular flow, and whether or not we could get across before a downstream obstacle. But it looked doable. We also had the added incentive of really having no other choice. Michael let me go first.

I stood at the top of the boulder, looking downstream. As if on cue, a strong wind blew in my face. I took a deep breath, started to run. I took six or seven large strides before I reached the edge, and I leapt as hard as I could, plunging feet first in the center of the river.

Underwater, the deafening roar muted, changed tone. The cold was as shocking as any I could remember, and I could feel the force of the current trying to turn my body in different directions, pulling my arms one way, my legs another. I sputtered to the surface and looked around, figured out which way was which, and started pulling for the other side as quickly as I could. I hauled myself out onto a steep pile of softball-sized rocks, which slid beneath my feet as I applied weight to them. Finally I stood completely out of the river, scrambled up a few steps, and turned to see how Michael was doing.

He was nearly to the rocks himself; he must have waited no more than a few seconds before following me into the torrent. Whether a sign of confidence or desperation, it all added up to the same thing now. He emerged from the swim no worse for the wear, and trotted up beside me.

I scanned the ground, searching for hope, and I found it in the mud just a few feet into the side canyon: a footprint, at worst a few days old. This was the side canyon, the escape we had been hoping for. We could just make out the faint impression of a trail switching back and forth up the slide area. Now there was nothing to it but the climb.

We hadn't had anything to eat or drink for hours, and the stress was beginning to show. Michael warmed to the idea of something as straightforward as a climb, one foot in front of the other. It was my own exhaustion that forced us to stop quite often; Michael was always ready to oblige. As we made our way up, we could sort of gauge our progress by looking at a nearly identical, but unscalable, side canyon on the other side of the Gunnison. Looking out as level as possible, we could tell ourselves we were a quarter of the way, a third of the way, half the way up. That progress could be measured at all was a great boost.

It was hot; the breezes we had become accustomed to in the main canyon were nowhere to be found, and although the sun was low, it was striking us fully in the backs as we humped up the rock field. Near the bottom, the "trail" cut back and forth across the kind of rocks I despised, great moving things that waited until you felt comfortable with them before slipping out from under your feet. Michael, again, was in his element, urging me on, somehow finding something to say that would make us laugh.

The climb went on and on, and the setting sun followed us up towards the rim. We squeezed between giant boulders and shimmied up them; we grabbed plants both firmly rooted and tenuous, inching higher. Birds of prey soared above us, then even with us, and finally just below us. Dust stuck to our sweat as we took on a color faintly reminiscent of the rocks, binding us to them. As we neared the top, we heard a rustling in a nearby tree, and stopped to listen. Suddenly, a sound of rushing air by our heads, and we turned to see a giant owl buzz past and perch on a sturdy branch.

The size of the animal was astounding; the quality of omen hung in the air. We couldn't decide whether it was a good omen, or a bad one; either way, the creature was fascinating. We watched it for ten minutes or so, the sudden movements of its head, the opening and closing of its eyes seeming to belong to the world of the artificial. I remember thinking how absurd it was, my perception that this robot-like owl was more out of place in this canyon than either of us. Finally it tired of us, or perhaps remembered what it had been doing before we came along, and it took off. I looked uphill, and saw that the treeline ended just above us. We took a last few steps, and were out.

We came out onto the rim, looking across at the world outside the canyon. The first thing we encountered was the back of a warning sign, something that amused both of us, and a dirt road. We weren't sure which way would lead to the ranger station, so we just cheerfully picked left, on the assumption that luck had to work in our favor at some point. We strolled down the road, laughing at how silly each of us looked, in shorts and life vests, walking down a deserted road in the backcountry of Colorado.

Remembering our Paria Canyon trip, Michael said: "You know, in twenty years, you and I are going to be talking just like this, slapping each other's backs and laughing, walking away from a burning airplane."

I had to agree, he was probably right.

Just up the road we ran into a ranger in his truck, a North Rim recluse named Jimmy. He told us he had been watching us climb out of the canyon; thinking we were a few climbers he had been expecting, he had been surprised when we emerged with lifejackets instead of ropes and harnesses. When we told him who we were, he laughed and said no one was expecting us to come out on this side.

Over water and jelly sandwiches graciously provided by our host back at the station, we drew where our packs were, more or less, on a piece of paper. Jimmy told us it was possible that someone could get down to them, but not to count on it. In all likelihood, we were among the last people to venture into the canyon that season; winter would hit soon, and the enormous changes in water volume associated with spring runoff would probably tear our stranded gear to pieces. We spent that night on the couch in the isolated ranger's station, while Jimmy radioed for a call to be placed to my wife, letting her know where we were. We drank gallons of water, and eventually fell into a hard, heavy, exhausted sleep.

21

We were strange looking objects. Our clothing and shoes were ragged and worn and with a luxuriant growth of beard and a covering of dirt acquired in the last few miles of our trip, we would hardly have been candidates for positions in polite society.

We had been obliged to swim the river, the water of which was as cold as ice, 76 times. The swimming was naturally fraught with great danger, it being necessary for us often to land on sharp points of rock where the water was flowing swiftly. We were bruised from head to foot. Each had lost at least fifteen pounds in the ten days' trip.

So ended this portion of the exploration and survey.

—A. Lincoln Fellows, 1901

SO WHO WRITES HISTORY?

Me, it would seem. Riding back from the North Rim, staring out the window of the truck as my wife drove Michael and me back towards showers and burgers, I found myself with little to say about the trip. Michael managed to get a few sentences off, and I tried my best to talk about the beauty of the canyon, the quiet moments and the powerful roar that was, as Fellows had described, constantly in our ears, and I found I came up short. The first few days were almost completely overpowered, at least in memory, by the extreme harshness of the last swim, the climb out. My mother-in-law took us all to lunch, and we were grateful, if not excellent conversationalists.

Physically, we weren't too beaten up. Torrence and Fellows, to say nothing of the Pelton party, had it much worse. We had a few scratches, some of them impressive; we had bruises all over, and we had sore legs, sore shoulders, and the odd blister on our feet. We were dirty, to be sure, but we were physiologically whole and more or less unscathed. What sat heavy on us was the emotional sense of loss, and the feeling that we got, as ranger Jimmy aptly put it, "spanked." A good word for it, really, full of all the right kind of connotations: arrogant, misbehaving children, given a sturdy dose of correction by, well, a parent. A big parent. Who knew better.

It's good to know, I suppose, that just because something was done a hundred years ago doesn't necessarily make it any less of an achievement. We go through school practically being taught to take for granted that things are easier today. Take Pythagoras, the greatest mind of his age; we learn the crowning achievement of his life's work by the time we're ten. The net result of this kind of thing is at least an undercurrent, if not an outright stated belief, that people were just dumber back then.

But a trip through the Black Canyon is no easier today than it was for Torrence and Fellows. Polypropylene and energy bars are great, but they don't make it any easier to haul a human body over a rock, or swim a rapid. And, truth be known, a stove or a sleeping bag, no matter how high-tech, really can't keep you warm if they're wrapped around a boulder in the middle of an icy river. It seems like an obvious thing, but it helps to be reminded by an occasional object lesson.

As for our gear, it's still down there. At the time of this writing, everything from Michael's camera equipment to our borrowed drybag was last seen by a few kayakers, who reported all of it shredded to bits by the force of the current and the sharp rocks. I felt bad about the mess, and hoped I could get down there in the spring to clean it all up a little.

The Black Canyon, of course, is also still there. Last I checked, visitor numbers at the rim were up, and a few more daring souls were trying their luck at river level as well. Fellows' great-granddaughter had mused about a centennial trip down old A. Lincoln's route sometime in 2001. I hoped she would fare well; I would wish her nothing more than sturdy shoes, good company, and a drought year. Perhaps not in that order.

I stumbled onto the Black Canyon. It became special to me, partly at least because it had been special to others. I came to know it as fully and as richly as anyone could, I think. I had dug around, read what I could, tried to get my brain wrapped around it. Finally I learned something about it that couldn't be written, as much as everyone who has come close to it has tried. For myself, the price of admission was relatively low.

I haven't been back into the place since it became a National Park, down inside or even to the rim, yet. I've stood in the nearby city of Montrose and looked at the backsides of the cliffs, at the green five-o'clock stubble of piñons against the brown dirt that looks like every other southwestern high desert. You can't see the rock walls from town, there's no evidence that just over the next rise is one of the last truly wild places in the country. From that angle, it could be any piece of land anywhere for hundreds of miles around, New Mexico maybe, or nearer to Utah. Nothing to distinguish it, on the face of things, from anywhere else.

22.

AS IT TURNS OUT, the story didn't manage to end there for me, not then. There was one more little tidbit, one more chapter, as it were.

Nearly a year and a half after Michael and I made our stagger to the rim, I received a phone call from a student at Western State, something of an extreme kayaker. He had found what seemed to be Michael's pack, or what was left of it. Ripped to shreds by the river's every season, and far downstream from where we had last seen it, the pack intrigued this young man enough to rifle through it. Back at the rim, he asked the rangers if they knew who might have left it there and, after he got back to school, he called me.

The pack, he said, was pretty much destroyed, and the clothing inside unsalvageable. A saturated down sleeping bag had been stained by rust from a point-and-shoot camera, broken open. Some kind of brightly colored foam padding had broken down, the "wacky noodles" last remains had spread across a sand bar.

The young man did take a couple of things from the pack. He carried out a slightly dented cookpan, since he had forgotten his own (I told him he was welcome to it). He also retrieved two intact film canisters, which he mailed to me. And I had them developed.

So here, dear reader, as a treat for making it this far, and as tribute to those who made it out of the Black Canyon with far less, are a few of the pictures Michael took. Enjoy them.